TAPE IT & WEAR IT

TAPE IT & WEAR IT

Richela Fabian Morgan

60 DUCT TAPE ACTIVITIES TO MAKE AND WEAR

BARRON'S

A QUINTET BOOK

First edition for the United States and Canada
published in 2014 by Barron's Educational Series, Inc.

All inquiries should be addressed to:
Barron's Educational Series, Inc.
250 Wireless Boulevard
Hauppauge, NY 11788
www.barronseduc.com

Library of Congress Control Number: 2014938664

ISBN: 978-1-4380-0519-5

QTT.DUC3

Conceived, designed, and produced by
Quintet Publishing Limited
4th Floor Sheridan House
114-116 Western Road
Hove BN3 1DD
United Kingdom

Project Editor: Caroline Elliker
Design: Rod Teasdale
Photography: Simon Pask
Lead Crafter: Gareth Butterworth
Assistant Crafter: Tessa Sillars Powell
Art Director: Michael Charles
Editorial Director: Emma Bastow
Publisher: Mark Searle

Printed in China by 1010 Printing International Ltd

Date of manufacture: July 2014

9 8 7 6 5 4 3 2 1

Contents

INTRODUCTION

Despite loving colors and patterns all my life, I am guilty of owning more than my share of monochromatic clothing. Instead I wear bright colors and patterns in the form of accessories and special one-off garments. I owned scarves that added a vibrant touch to an otherwise muted dress or pantsuit. I also had a vest made of mini multi-colored bow ties that I wore with tuxedo pants (sartorial nightmare? I think not!). My monochromatic clothing habit actually serves as the foundation for bold fashion statements.

As a crafter, I've discovered that duct tape in its recent incarnation lends itself to being the fashion statement. Designers are already making neckties, hats, and belts (to name a few) in houndstooth, paisley, gingham, argyle, and chevron. It is not mere coincidence that duct tape is offered in patterns with the same names. We are meant to treat duct tape like fabric more than ever, and to create wearable items from the stuff not just for shock value. Duct tape is fashion couture.

Sometimes less is definitely more, duct tape jewelry can be an addition that solicits silent accolades from onlookers—a pair of cufflinks, a bracelet or ring. But if you do want to "go big," a duct tape skirt is an easy no-sew garment to make. And if you can make a pattern, then the sky is the limit for your imagination.

This book contains wearable duct tape crafts for almost every part of your body. Like with my two previous duct tape craft books, *Tape It & Make It* and *Tape It & Make More*, these projects should serve as a springboard for your own creativity. Follow the instructions provided, make the projects as written, and then experiment with colors or size. Fashion is such a personal thing; it is an expression of our individuality, conscious or not.

Okay, now. Let's get started!

TOOLS

The following tools are a basic kit for most projects:

- Self-healing cutting mat, size 12 in. x 36 in. (30 cm x 90 cm)
- Craft knife (size 10), and extra blades
- Metal ruler with cork backing, 12 in. (30 cm) long
- Metal ruler with cork backing, 24 in. (60 cm) long
- Scissors
- Detail scissors

TIPS ON MAKING PATTERNS

When measuring your body:
1. Always use a flexible tape measure.
2. Record measurements while wearing your usual undergarments.
3. Measurements should be snug, not tight.
4. Leave ample room for ease of movement.
5. Measure the fullest part when measuring any section (e.g., chest, hips).

When making a pattern:
1. Newspaper or thin magazine paper is the best material to use. Any other type of paper is either too stiff or too flimsy.
2. Piece together the newspaper into a large piece before drawing out your measurements for larger garments.
3. Be aware of how much room you need to accommodate not only ease of movement but also the design of your garment.
4. If your garment needs several pattern parts, be sure to label each one properly.
5. Draw the pattern first in pencil, and then re-trace it with a single solid line in marker.
6. Cut out the pattern with scissors or a craft knife.

When tracing a pattern onto duct tape:
1. It is best to use a grease pencil, also known as a China marker. Markers and pen are hard to remove from duct tape, and it is hard to see the lines if you use a pencil.
2. Be aware of which is the inside and outside of your fabric before you begin.

REMEMBER: patterns can be reused, so don't throw them out!

TIPS ON STRIPS

On saving the bits on the end of a roll: I often have rolls of tape that do not amount to a full-scale project. To save space, I'll cut the usable part of the roll—usually a few inches, centimeters or feet—and place it on a piece of parchment paper. I can then store them flat in an accordion folder. If my strip is too small, I'll save it for a glass marker or key chain project. But if there is enough, I'll start sketching out ideas for accessories.

On making a double-sided strip: Don't try to handle the strip with overly dry hands. It's quite possible to rip off some skin (ouch!), so moisturize your hands with a bit of lotion first. When folding the strip onto itself, hold it with your fingernails as much as possible and work in quick motions.

On folding strips lengthwise: Whether it's folding in half or thirds, work one section at a time. Hold down the sticky side with a fingernail rather than a fingertip while folding the opposite side. And no matter how careful you are, the folded strip will curl—this is not a failure! This is just something that occurs and is perfectly normal.

CREATING DUCT TAPE FABRICS

"SQUARING UP"

When making duct tape fabrics, you will need to "square up" the edges. This means that the edges of the fabric should be neatly trimmed using a metal ruler and craft knife, and that the edges should be perpendicular to each other. Use the grid on the self-healing cutting mat to ensure that each corner is exactly 90 degrees.

AVOIDING BUBBLES OR BUMPS

It is important to clean the cutting mat before laying down any tape. Wipe down the mat with a damp cloth; wipe again with a dry cloth. Run your hand across it to check for any stuck-on debris and wipe again if needed.

VARIETIES OF DUCT TAPE FABRIC

One-Sided Layered Fabric

For this fabric, the reverse side will remain sticky unless a thin cotton handkerchief, bandana, or polyester scarf is affixed to it to act as a lining.

1. Unwind the roll of tape across the surface of a cutting mat to the desired length. Cut off this strip with scissors.
2. Lay another strip of tape across the cutting mat, overlapping the first strip by ⅛ in. (3 mm). Repeat until you reach the desired overall size.
3. Square up the fabric. From one corner, gently peel off the tape across the diagonal to prevent the pieces from coming apart.

1

2

3

5

Double-Sided Layered Fabric

This duct tape fabric is slightly thicker than the single layer. For a two-tone look, use two different colors for the fabric's front and back sides—this not only looks more playful, it also allows you to make your project reversible.

1. Cut a piece of duct tape and place it on the cutting mat, sticky side facing up. Fold down the top edge to make a ¼ in. (6 mm) border.
2. Lay the second strip of tape sticky side down, across the first strip so they overlap by ¼ in. (6 mm) on both their top and bottom edges.
3. Flip it over so that the sticky side of the bottom strip is facing up. Lay another strip of tape, sticky side down, across the bottom strip, overlapping by the same measure. Repeat this step until you reach your desired height.
4. Once you've reached the desired height, flip the fabric over so that the last strip is at the bottom, with the sticky side facing up.
5. Fold over the bottom edge so that the sticky side is completely covered, then square up the fabric.

Woven Fabric

This simple up-and-over technique allows you to create checkered patterns, and also "boogie-woogie" Piet Mondrian-type squares. Or if you use a single color, the fabric takes on a more tactile quality which really transforms the duct tape into something else entirely.

1. Lay strips of tape horizontally across the cutting mat, sticky side down. Leave a slight gap between each strip, but make sure that each is no greater than $1/16$ in. (1.5 mm).
2. Starting on the right edge, pull up every other strip and gently double them back on themselves. Then place a strip of duct tape vertically down, across those strips that remain stuck down. Replace the pulled-up horizontal strips on top of the vertical strip.
3. Pull the alternate horizontal strips up, starting on the right side and working toward the left. Vertically place another strip of duct tape to the immediate left edge of the first vertical strip, as close to it as possible without actually touching. Then, replace the lifted horizontal strips on the top of the new vertical strip. Repeat this step until you reach the desired size of the fabric.
4. Gently pry up the fabric's lower right corner, and pull it up off the cutting mat in a diagonal motion toward its upper left corner.
5. Put down the fabric with its sticky side facing upward. Cover the sticky surface with a thin cotton material, like an old t-shirt or bandana. Use your hands to smooth out any air bubbles, then square-up the edges of the fabric, and flip it over to reveal the front side of the finished woven fabric.

2

3

4

5

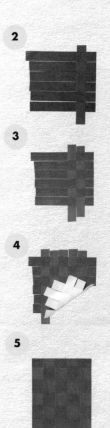

CHAPTER 1

Bracelets, Rings, & Things

Sometimes it's the little things that cause the most commotion. A duct tape bracelet seems to be my biggest attention grabber yet. When a certain dark wood grain pattern became available, I just had to make a faux wood duct tape bangle. The compliments started pouring in, and not once did I need to reveal it was made of duct tape. This experience made me realize how duct tape can be easily incorporated into the design without overwhelming it. As it only takes a little duct tape to make something for your wrist or hand, no one seems to question what the material is.

The projects in this chapter require some twisting, rolling, and fine cutting. You'll need a pair of pliers, wire cutters, hemp cord, and clasps. And when you are instructed to add oil (any type will do) to bamboo skewers, don't imagine yourself at a barbecue grill! No, you are creating fabulous accessories from duct tape.

Materials

» Flower wallpaper print duct tape
» 22 gauge floral wire

Additional tools

» Wire cutters

1. **Wraparound Bracelet**

1 Cut a 20 in. (51 cm) strip of tape. Fold it in half lengthwise, but leave a ¼ in. (6 mm) wide sticky section exposed along the top edge.

2 Fold the double-sided section only lengthwise in half, leaving the sticky section out. Then fold the sticky section over. You've created a loop inside this bracelet band.

3 Along the bottom edge, cut triangles into the band. Each triangle should be ¼ in. (6 mm) high and ¼ in. (6 mm) wide at the base. There should be ¼ in. (6 mm) space between each triangle.

4 Cut a 17 in. (43 cm) piece of wire. Push it through the inside loop of the band so it rubs against the cut section.

5 Fold the wire over the band at one end. Slowly curve the band into a spiral that will fit around your wrist. Fold the wire over the opposite end to hold it in place.

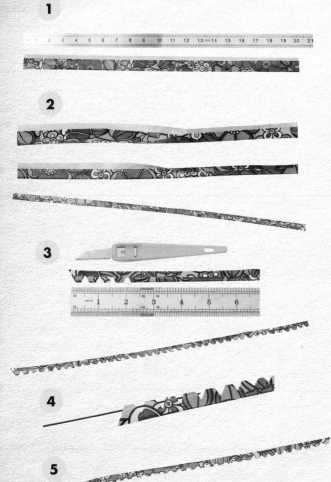

2. Cuff Bracelet

Materials

» Cotton candy duct tape
» 22 gauge floral wire

Additional tools

» Wire cutters
» Flat nose pliers
» Thick needle or awl

1 Cut two 7–8 in. (18–20 cm) long strips. Take one strip and place it lengthwise on your workspace with the sticky side facing down. Take the second strip and cut it in half lengthwise. Place each half strip at the top and bottom edges of the first strip so it overlaps by ½ in. (1.25 cm). Flip over so the sticky side is facing up. This is the bracelet band.

2 Cut two 8 in. (20 cm) long pieces of wire. Place each piece, ½ in. (1.25 cm) from each edge, at the top and bottom of the assembled tape strips. Fold over the top and bottom so the wire defines the edges of the bracelet. Set aside.

3 Cut a 12 in. (30.5 cm) long strip of tape. Place it on your workspace lengthwise with the sticky side facing up. Cut a 13 in. (33 cm) long strip of tape and cut it down to ½ in. (1.25 cm) wide. Place this second strip on top of the first strip and directly in the horizontal center, sticky side facing down.

4 Fold the strip in half, bringing the bottom edge up to meet the top edge. You should have a loop along the folded edge.

5 Cut a 14 in. (36 cm) piece of wire. Pass it all the way through the loop of the folded tape strip.

1

2

3

4

5

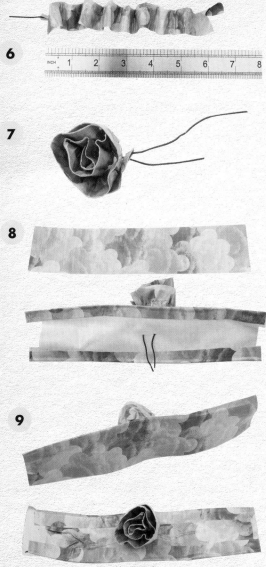

6 Hold one end of the wire with pliers. Push the tape from the opposite end toward the end with the pliers, crinkling the tape to 6 in. (15 cm) long.

7 Carefully twirl the wired tape into a spiral to create a flower. Bend the wire on both ends to hold the flower shape. Trim the ends of the wire to leave 1 in. (2.5 cm) tails of wire. Set aside.

8 Using the thick needle, poke two holes in the center of the bracelet band. Take the flower and pass the wire tails through the holes of the band starting from the non-sticky side. Fold the wires down so the flower is secured to the band.

9 Cut an 8 in. (20 cm) strip of tape. Cover the reverse side of the band.

10 At the outer edges of the band, round off the corners with a pair of scissors.

11 Fold the band edges inward. Then curve the entire bracelet into a cuff shape.

3. Faux Woven Bracelet

Materials

» Black duct tape
» Gold duct tape
» Flower wallpaper print duct tape
» ¾ in. (2 cm) wide nail file or tongue depressor
» Velcro® tab

1 Cut a 12 in. (30.5 cm) strip of black tape. Cut it in half lengthwise. Take one of the half strips and fold it in thirds to make a band approximately ¼ in. (6 mm) wide.

2 Cut the remaining strip of black tape in half vertically. Take one of the strips and place it on top of the center part of the band. Set aside the remaining strip.

3 Cut a 6 in. (12.5 cm) strip of gold tape and a 6 in. (12.5 cm) strip of flower wallpaper tape. Cut each strip lengthwise into eight equal pieces, then cut again in half vertically. You should have 32 strips (16 gold, 16 flower) measuring 3 in. (7.5 cm) wide by ¼ in. (6 mm) tall.

4 Using the nail file as a spacer, place 4–5 gold strips consecutively on top of the black center strip (which you placed along the center of the band in step 2), at 45-degree angles.

5 Again, using the nail file as a spacer, place 4–5 flower strips consecutively on top and in the opposite direction of the gold strips so they form 90-degree angles where they intersect.

6 Place gold strips between the existing ones on the band. You are "weaving" these strips with the flower strips.

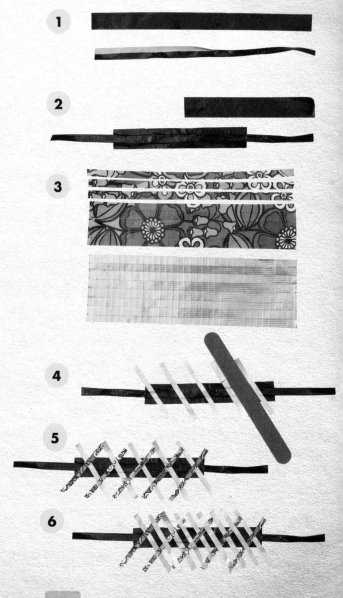

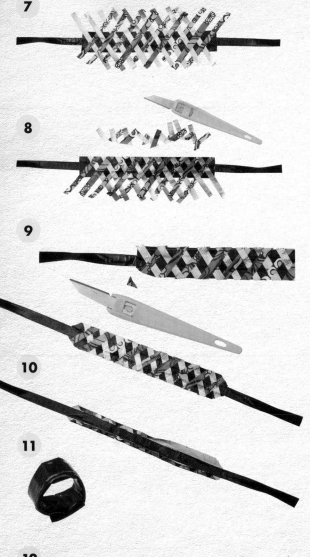

7 Place flower strips between the existing ones on the band. You have now completed your duct tape faux weave.

8 Cut off the excess bits of the strips at the top and bottom.

9 At the left and right edges where the woven section meets the band, cut off the corners at 45-degree angles.

10 Flip over so the sticky side is facing up. Fold over the edges of the woven section.

11 From the remaining black strip made in step 2, cut a piece ½ in. (1.25 cm) wide by 1 in. (2.5 cm) high. Fold it in thirds. Make a loop by placing the ends together. Cut another small piece of black tape and use it to secure the ends of the loop.

12 Place the loop through one of the band arms, ½ in. (1.25 cm) from the woven section. Fold the arm in so it touches the reverse of the bracelet. Cut another small piece of black tape and secure the arm in place.

13 On the remaining arm place a Velcro® tab.

4. Bead & Knot Bracelet

Materials

» Blue and green plaid duct tape
» Brown hemp cord
» Two jump rings
» Clasp

Additional tools

» Bamboo skewer
» Oil
» Flat nose pliers

1 Cut a 12 in. (30.5 cm) strip of tape. Cut it in half lengthwise. Cut each half strip in half again along the diagonal to give four narrow triangular strips.

2 Take one of the triangular strips and place it vertically (with the apex at the top and base at the bottom) on your workspace, sticky side facing up. Fold the bottom edge inward ¼ in. (6 mm) as shown, making the outer angles of the base an equal distance and into an isosceles triangle. The apex of the triangle should now lie directly in the center opposite of the base.

3 Take the bamboo skewer and rub oil on it. Place it at the bottom of the triangular strip. Roll skewer upwards, and as you do so, roll the strip around it. This is a bead. When fully rolled, the apex of the strip should end up in the center of the bead. Push the bead off the skewer.

1

2

3

4 Repeat steps 2 and 3 to make four beads in total. Be sure to rub oil on the skewer before making each bead.

5 Repeat steps 1–4 so that you have eight beads.

6 Cut a 28 in. (71 cm) piece of hemp cord and fold in half to 14 in. (35.5 cm) length. Tie a double-knot 2 in. (5 cm) from the end. Place a bead through the open end of the cord and push it through until it is stopped by the double-knot. Tie another double-knot on the opposite side of the bead, holding it in place.

7 Place the other beads through the cord. After each bead is strung through, tie a double-knot.

8 Tie a jump ring to each end of the cord. Then use pliers to attach a clasp to one of the jump rings. Trim off any excess cord.

6

7

5. Long Bead Bracelet

1 Cut a 3 in. (7.5 cm) strip of tape. Place on your workspace in the vertical position. Fold the bottom edge inward ¼ in. (6 mm). Rub oil on the bamboo skewer and place it at the bottom of the strip. Roll skewer upwards and as you do so roll the strip around it. This is a bead.

2 Repeat step 1 until you have a total of 24 beads.

3 Cut a 52 in. (132 cm) piece of wire. Place all the beads through the wire leaving equal wire tails at each end. Fold the wire at each space between the beads in a "Z" formation.

Materials

» Leopard print duct tape
» 30 gauge jewelry wire
» Four crimping beads
» Jump ring
» Clasp

Additional tools

» Bamboo skewer
» Oil
» Wire cutters
» Flat nose pliers

1

2

3

4 Cut another 52 in. (132 cm) piece of wire. At the first bead, push the wire through the opening that does NOT have a wire tail sticking out. Then snake the wire through the other beads in a "Z" formation, going the opposite direction of the first wire. This should hold the beads together side by side.

5 Pull the wires taut and twist them at each end. Place a crimping bead at each end of the wires and flatten with pliers.

6 On one end, place the wire through a crimping bead. Wrap the wires around a jump ring, and then place them through the crimping bead again. Flatten the bead with pliers and cut off any excess wire.

7 On the remaining end, place the wire through a crimping bead. Push the wires through a clasp, and then place them through the crimping bead again. Flatten the bead with pliers and cut off any excess wire.

4

5

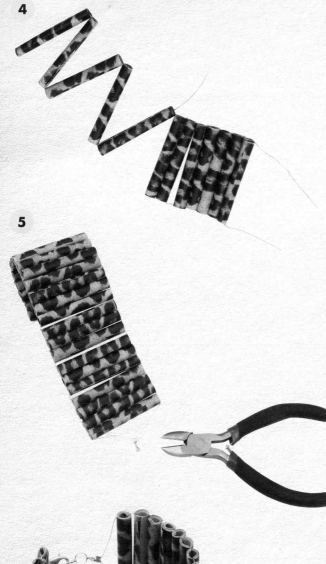

6. Bangle

1 Cut two 9 ½ in. (24 cm) strips of Brazilian rosewood tape. Cut one of the strips horizontally in half. Take one of the half strips and place it on the bottom edge of the whole strip to overlap by ¼ in. (6 mm). Take the remaining half strip and place it on the top edge of the whole strip to overlap by ¼ in. (6 mm). Flip over so the sticky side is facing up.

2 Cut a 9 ½ in. (24 cm) strip of the second color tape. Cut two ½ in. (1.25 cm) wide strips from this. Place these strips horizontally on top of the assembled rosewood tape strips, one at the top and the other at the bottom, ¼ in. (6 mm) from the edges.

3 Fold over the top and bottom edges ½ in. (1.25 cm). You are creating a non-sticky loop at the edges of the bracelet band. After folding over the top and bottom edges, the overall height of the bracelet band should be 2 ½ in. (6.5 cm).

4 Cut a 9 ½ in. (24 cm) strip of rosewood tape. Place it horizontally on top of the bracelet band, covering any exposed sticky surface.

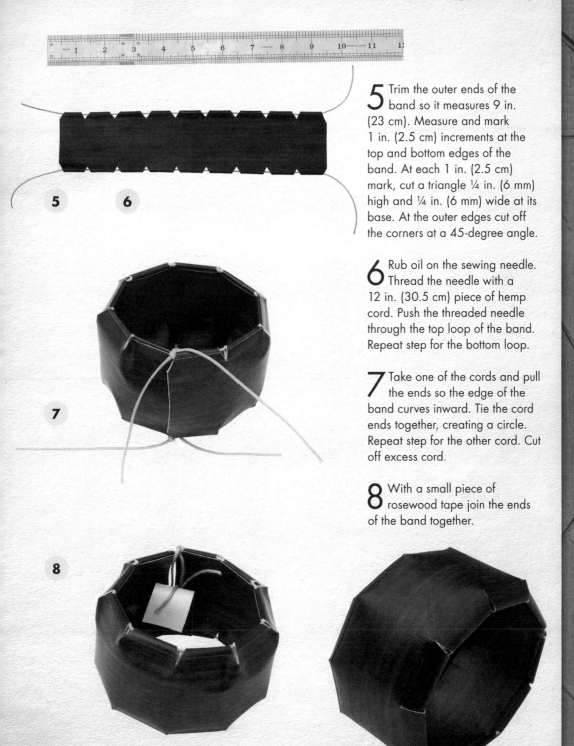

5 Trim the outer ends of the band so it measures 9 in. (23 cm). Measure and mark 1 in. (2.5 cm) increments at the top and bottom edges of the band. At each 1 in. (2.5 cm) mark, cut a triangle ¼ in. (6 mm) high and ¼ in. (6 mm) wide at its base. At the outer edges cut off the corners at a 45-degree angle.

6 Rub oil on the sewing needle. Thread the needle with a 12 in. (30.5 cm) piece of hemp cord. Push the threaded needle through the top loop of the band. Repeat step for the bottom loop.

7 Take one of the cords and pull the ends so the edge of the band curves inward. Tie the cord ends together, creating a circle. Repeat step for the other cord. Cut off excess cord.

8 With a small piece of rosewood tape join the ends of the band together.

7. Chunky Bracelet

1 Cut a 3 in. (7.5 cm) strip of tape. Place on your workspace in the vertical position. Fold the bottom edge inward ¼ in. (6 mm). Rub oil on the bamboo skewer and place it at the bottom of the strip. Roll skewer upwards, and as you do so roll the strip around it. This is a bead.

2 Repeat step 1 until you have eight beads. Set aside.

3 Cut four 4 in. (10 cm) strips of tape. Turn them over so the sticky side is facing up. With a pen, measure and mark 1 in. (2.5 cm) in from the left and right edges.

4 Place one bead vertically on each pair of 1 in. (2.5 cm) marks. There should be two beads on each strip.

5 Fold over the left and right edges of each strip so they meet in the middle. With a fingernail, press the tape down around the beads inside. These are the rectangle plates.

6 Rub oil on the sewing needle and thread with a 24 in. (61 cm) piece of hemp cord. Push the threaded needle through one of the beads inside in a rectangle plate. Pull the thread diagonally across and push the needle through the second inside bead.

Materials

» Denim duct tape
» Hemp cord
» Four crimping beads
» Small jump ring
» Three medium jump rings
» Clasp

Additional tools

» Bamboo skewer and oil
» 3 in. (7.5 cm), or longer, sewing needle
» Flat nose pliers

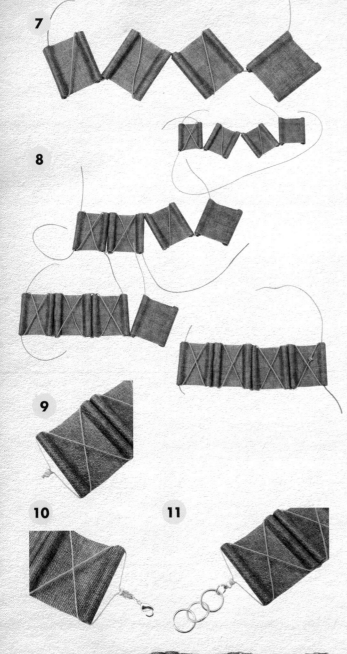

7 Take another rectangle plate and push the threaded needle through one of the inner beads. Pull the thread diagonally across and push the needle through the second inside bead. Repeat step for the remaining beads.

8 Cut another 24 in. (61 cm) piece of hemp cord. Repeat steps 6 and 7 but start with the opposite end of the first inner bead. As you pull the thread diagonally across each plate, you will be creating an "X".

9 Pull the cord ends taut at one end. Place them through a crimping bead and pull the bead down as far as it can go. Flatten the bead with pliers. Repeat step on the opposite end.

10 At one end, place the cords through a crimping bead. Push the cords through a clasp, and then place through the crimping bead again. Flatten the bead with pliers and cut off any excess cord.

11 On the remaining end, place the cords through a crimping bead. Push the cords through a small jump ring, and then place them through the crimping bead again. Flatten the bead with pliers and cut off any excess cord. Attach three medium jump rings to the small jump ring.

8. Rope Bangle

Materials

» White duct tape
» Gold duct tape

1 Cut a 10 in. (25 cm) strip of white tape. Cut the strip lengthwise in half then cut each half strip lengthwise in half again. You will have four ½ in. (1.25 cm) wide strips.

1

2

3

2 Fold each of these strips in thirds to make ropes.

3 Cut a 3 in. (7.5 cm) strip of gold tape. Cut the strip lengthwise in half, then cut each half strip vertically into three 1 in. (2.5 cm) pieces. You will have six 1 in. (2.5 cm) by ½ in. (1.25 cm) pieces.

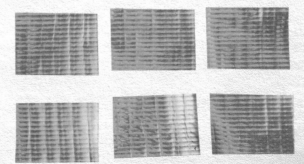

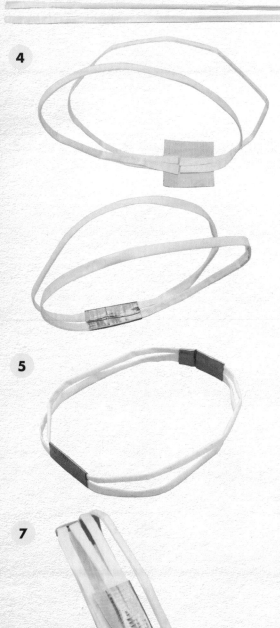

4 Take one of the gold tape pieces and place it on the workspace with the sticky side facing up. Take two of the white ropes and place one set of the ends on top of the gold tape. Pull the opposite ends of the ropes around and place them on the gold tape, forming a circle. Fold the gold tape over the rope ends to secure the circle.

5 On the direct opposite side of the circle place and fold another piece of gold tape over the two ropes.

6 Repeat steps 4 and 5.

7 Place one set of ropes on top of the other. Be sure the gold sections are lined up together, at 0 degrees and 180 degrees. With the remaining gold tape, attach the inner ropes of each set together, at 90 degrees and 270 degrees.

9. Round Double Panel Cufflinks

1 Cut a 4 in. (10 cm) strip of Brazilian rosewood tape. Fold it in half to make a double-sided strip. Using the circles stencil, trace four ⅝ in. (1.5 cm) diameter circles. Cut out the circles with a well-oiled pair of scissors.

2 Cut a 4 in. (10 cm) strip of orange linen tape. Fold it in half to make a double-sided strip. Using the circles stencil, trace four ½ in. (1.2 cm) diameter circles. Cut out the circles with a well-oiled pair of scissors. Place them on top of the rosewood circles.

3 Cut a 2 in. (5 cm) strip of white tape. Fold it in half to make a double-sided strip. Using the circles stencil, trace four ⁵⁄₁₆ in. (8 mm) diameter circles. Cut out the circles with a well-oiled pair of scissors. Place them on top of the other circles.

4 Center each set of circles. Poke a hole in the middle of each set with a thick sewing needle.

Materials

» Brazilian rosewood duct tape
» Orange linen duct tape
» White duct tape
» Dark brown hemp cord

Additional tools

» Circles stencil
» Pen
» Thick sewing needle

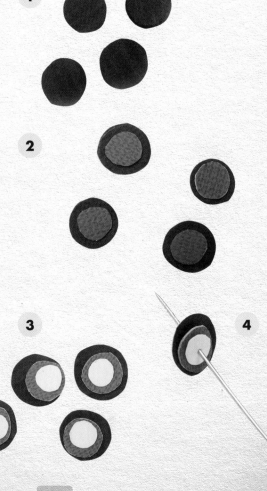

5

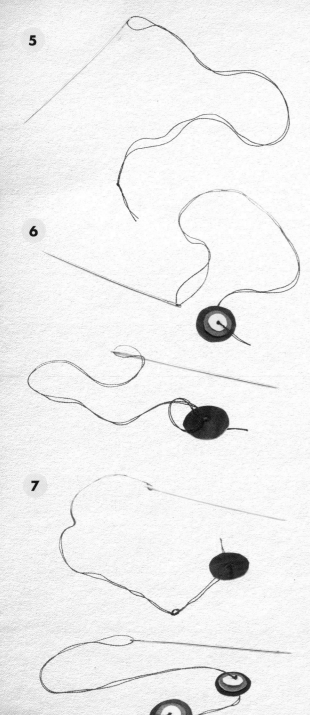

6

7

5 Cut an 18 in. (46 cm) piece of hemp cord. Thread one end through the eye of the sewing needle and pull it so that the needle is halfway on the cord. Tie a knot 1 in. (2.5 cm) from the ends of the cord.

6 Push the threaded needle through the front (white) side of one circle set. Pull the thread until the reverse side of the circle set reaches the knot. Tie a knot against the reverse side to hold it in place.

7 From the knot on the reverse side, measure 1 in. (2.5 cm) and tie a knot. Push the needle through the reverse side of a second set of circles and move it until it reaches the knot. Tie another knot on the front side to hold it in place. Trim the cord 1/8 in. (3 mm) from the knot. This is a cufflink.

8 Using the existing threaded needle, repeat steps 5–7 for the second cufflink.

9 Trim the cord ends of the cufflinks to 1/8 in. (3 mm).

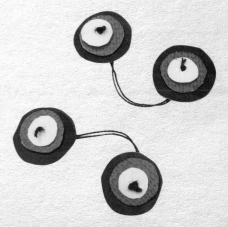

10. Square Double Panel Cufflinks

Materials

» Grass duct tape
» Gold duct tape
» White duct tape
» Brown hemp cord

Additional tools

» Thick sewing needle

1 Cut a 2 in. (5 cm) strip of grass tape. Fold it in half to make a double-sided strip. Cut out four ½ in. (1.25 cm) squares.

2 Cut a 10 in. (25 cm) strip of gold tape. Cut it down to ¼ in. (6 mm) wide. Set the extra tape aside. Cut the strip down again into four 2 ½ in. (6.5 cm) strips.

3 Wrap a gold strip around the middle of each grass square.

4 Cut a 10 in. (25 cm) strip of white tape. Cut it down to ¼ in. (6 mm) wide. Discard the extra tape. Cut the strip down again into four 2 ½ in. (6.5 cm) strips.

1

2

3

4

5 Wrap a white strip around the middle of each square, crossing the gold strip to form a "+".

6 Take the extra tape from step 2. Cut it down to ⅛ in. (3 mm) wide. Cut the strip down again into four 2 ½ in. (6.5 cm) strips.

7 Wrap a gold strip around the middle of each square, centered on the white strip.

8 Poke a hole in the middle of each square with a thick sewing needle.

9 Cut an 18 in. (46 cm) piece of hemp cord. Thread one end through the eye of the needle and pull it so the needle is halfway along the cord. Tie a knot 1 in. (2.5 cm) from the ends of the cord.

10 Push the threaded needle through one square. Pull the thread until the reverse side of the square reaches the knot. Tie a knot against the reverse side to hold it in place.

11 From the knot on the reverse side, measure 1 in. (2.5 cm) and tie a knot. Push the needle through a second square and move it until it reaches the knot. Tie another knot on the front side to hold it in place. Trim the cord approximately ⅛ in. (3 mm) from the knot. This is a cufflink.

12 Using the existing threaded needle, repeat steps 9–11 to make the second cufflink.

13 Trim the cord ends of the cufflinks to ⅛ in. (3 mm).

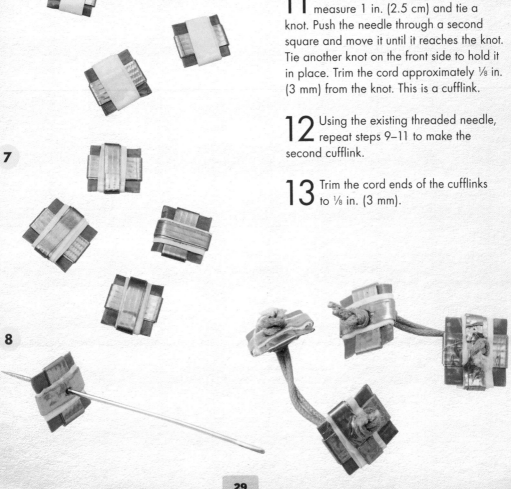

5

7

8

11. Rose Ring

Materials

» Red duct tape

1 Cut a 10 in. (25 cm) strip of red tape. Fold the strip lengthwise by pulling up the bottom edge. Leave ¼ in. (6 mm) wide sticky section along the top edge.

2 Place the strip on the worktable in the vertical position. Start rolling the strip upward from the bottom. As you roll the strip, pinch the sticky side and progressively loosen the spiral on the opposite side. Pinching the sticky side will hold the spiral as your roll the strip. Loosening the spiral as you roll will give you the shape of the rose.

3 Cut a 4 ½ in. (11.5 cm) strip of tape. Cut it in half lengthwise. Take one half of the strip and roll it around the bottom of the rose, forming a short stem.

1

2

3

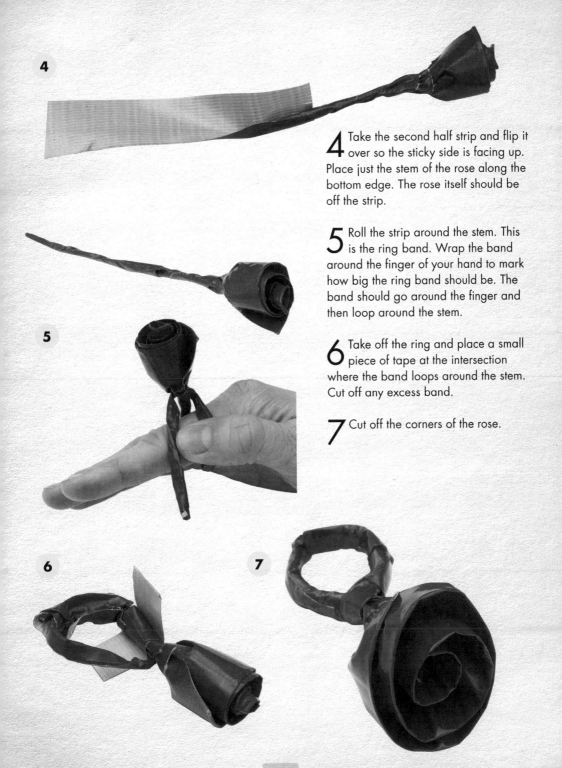

4 Take the second half strip and flip it over so the sticky side is facing up. Place just the stem of the rose along the bottom edge. The rose itself should be off the strip.

5 Roll the strip around the stem. This is the ring band. Wrap the band around the finger of your hand to mark how big the ring band should be. The band should go around the finger and then loop around the stem.

6 Take off the ring and place a small piece of tape at the intersection where the band loops around the stem. Cut off any excess band.

7 Cut off the corners of the rose.

12. Single Bead Ring

Materials

» Gummy bears duct tape
» 22 gauge floral wire

Additional tools

» Bamboo skewer
» Oil
» Wire cutters

1 Cut a 14 in. (35.5 cm) strip of tape. Cut it in half lengthwise. Set one half strip aside.

2 Line up the edges of the remaining half strip with the grid lines on your cutting mat in the vertical position. Cut out an isosceles triangle with a 1 in. (2.5 cm) base by measuring the halfway point at the top edge, and angling your ruler to the left and right bottom corners. Discard excess tape.

3 Rub oil on the bamboo skewer. Flip over the triangle so the sticky side is facing up. At the base fold the bottom edge in ¼ in. (6 mm). Place the skewer on top of the folded edge. Roll the triangle around the skewer.

4 As you roll the triangle around the skewer, the bead will form in the center. Once the rolling is finished, the tip of the triangle should be at the center of the bead. Push the bead off the skewer.

5 Using the remaining half-strip of tape from step 1, cut a 4 in. (10cm) strip and place it on the worktable with the sticky side facing up. Cut a 6 in. (15 cm) piece of wire and place it lengthwise along the bottom edge of the tape strip. Roll the tape around the wire.

6 Place the ends of the wrapped wire in opposite ends of the bead. This is the ring. Place the ring on your finger and pull the wire ends until you get the desired size.

7 Take the ring off and trim any excess wire. Squeeze the bead to flatten it on top of the wires inside.

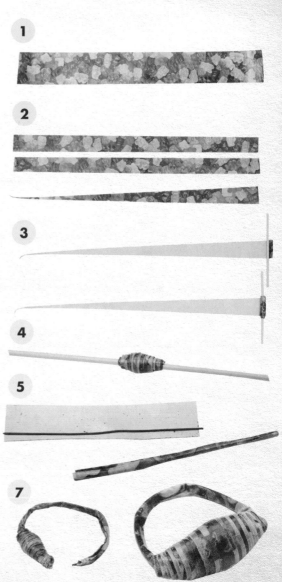

Materials

» Multi-color chevron duct tape
» White duct tape
» Gold duct tape

13. Square Ring

1 Make a double-sided piece of multi-color chevron tape at least 1 ½ in. (4 cm) long. Cut it down to a 1 in. (2.5 cm) square.

2 Cut a 10 in. (25 cm) strip of white tape and trim it down to ¾ in. (2 cm) wide. Discard extra tape. Wrap the strip around the chevron square.

3 Cut a 10 in. (25 cm) strip of gold tape and trim it down to ½ in. (1.25 cm) wide. Set aside the extra tape. Wrap the strip around the middle of the white section of the chevron square.

4 From the remaining gold tape, cut a 3 in. (7.5 cm) strip and fold it into thirds. This is the ring band.

5 Place the band on top of the wrapped chevron square. Be sure it is centered. With a small piece of gold tape, secure the band to the chevron square.

6 Take the ends of the band and overlap them to make a circle. Place a small piece of gold tape on the overlapping ends to hold the circle in place.

1

2

3
4

5

6

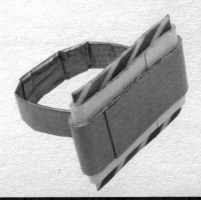

14. Heart Ring

Materials

» Red duct tape
» Gold duct tape

Additional tools

» Cotton pad or paper towel
» Small piece of parchment paper
» Pencil

1 Cut out a heart from the cotton pad to fit inside a ½ in. (1.25 cm) square. Cut a 2 in. (5 cm) strip of gold tape. Place the strip lengthwise on the worktable with the sticky side face up. Place the heart on the left half of the strip. Pull the right edge of the tape and fold the tape over the heart. Trim the excess tape around the heart leaving an ⅛ in. (3 mm) border.

2 Place the heart on top of the parchment paper and trace around it with a pencil. Remove the heart and cover the paper with red tape. With a pair of well-oiled scissors, cut out the heart shape but ⅛ in. (3 mm) smaller all around. This is the heart sticker.

3 Remove the parchment paper from the back of the sticker. Place it in the center of the gold heart.

4 Cut a 3 in. (7.5 cm) strip of gold tape. Cut the strip lengthwise in half. Fold one of the half strips from the bottom, about ⅛ in. (3 mm) and keep folding up lengthwise until a band is made.

5 Place the heart on the worktable with the red side facing down. Place the folded band in the horizontal position on top of the heart. Take the remaining strip of gold tape and cut it in half lengthwise. Use one of the half strips to adhere the band to the back of the heart and trim off any excess.

6 Take the ends of the band and overlap them to make a circle. Use the remaining gold tape half strip on the overlapping ends to hold the circle in place and trim excess.

Materials

» Blue surf flower duct tape
» Spool of 30 gauge jewelry wire.

Additional tools

» Wire cutters
» Flat nose pliers

15. Spiral Ring

1 Cut an 8 in. (20.5 cm) strip of tape. Cut strip in half lengthwise. Set aside one of the half strips.

2 Place the remaining half strip on the worktable sticky side facing up. Take the spool of wire and pull out an 8 ½ in. (21.5 cm) section. DO NOT cut. Place the wire lengthwise along the bottom edge of the strip so that ½ in. (1.25 cm) sticks out at one side. Roll the strip around the wire.

3 Bend the ½ in. (1.25 cm) wire tail down on one side. The opposite end should still be attached to the wire spool. Hold the wire spool end of the rolled tape with pliers and start to wrap it around itself in a spiral.

4 After each revolution wrap the wire around the rolled tape. Do this until you have a flat spiral disk.

5 Cut the wire 10 in. (25 cm) from where the spool is attached. Weave the wire through the reverse side of the disk once.

6 Using the extra tape from step 1, cut a 2 in. (5 cm) strip. Place it on the worktable sticky side facing up. Place the wire (attached to the disk) along the bottom edge of the strip, ensuring that it touches the disk. Roll the strip around the wire.

7 Push the end of the wire through the opposite side of the disk and pull it all the way through until stopped at the rolled tape section to form the ring band. Begin wrapping the wire around each revolution of the spiral directly opposite the existing ones, and once complete cut off any excess wire.

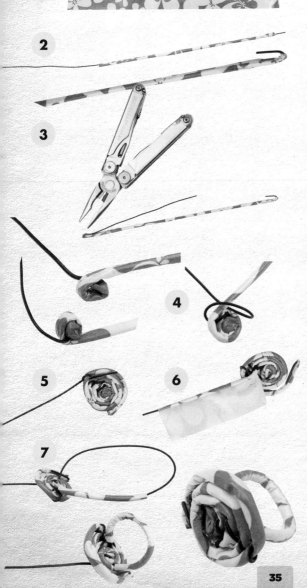

1
2
3
4
5
6
7

16. Letter Ring

Materials

» Sour apple linen duct tape
» White duct tape

Additional tools

» Circles stencil
» Parchment paper
» Pencil

 Cut a 2 in. (5 cm) strip of sour apple linen tape. Fold in half to create a double-sided piece. Place the stencil on top and trace a 13⁄16 in. (2 cm) diameter circle. Cut out circle with scissors and set aside.

2 On a piece of parchment paper trace four circles each slightly smaller than the last, with the largest having a diameter of ¾ in. (1.9 cm) and the smallest a diameter of ⅝ in. (1.6 cm).

3 Place a strip of sour apple linen tape on the paper so it covers the circles. Flip it over so you can see the traced circles through the paper. Cut out circles with well-oiled scissors.

4 Remove the paper from the cut circles and place them centered on top of the set aside 13⁄16 in. (2 cm) circle in size order from largest to smallest.

2

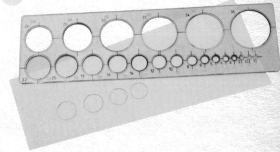

3

4

5

6

9

10

5 Trace a ⅝ in. (1.6 cm) diameter circle onto a piece of parchment paper. Choose a chunky style font and draw a letter inside the circle. Place a piece of white tape on the paper so it covers the letter. Flip it over so you can see the letter through the paper. Cut out the letter.

6 Remove the paper from the back of the letter and place it centered on top of the circles stack.

7 Cut a 3 in. (7.5 cm) strip of sour apple linen tape. Fold in half lengthwise. Trim down with scissors to ½ in. (1.25 cm) wide. This is the band.

8 Place the circles on the worktable with the letter side facing down. Place the band in the horizontal position on top of the circles.

9 Take a ½ in. (1.25 cm) strip of sour apple linen tape and use to adhere the band to the back of the circles. Trim off any excess tape around the circles and band so it is not visible once it is flipped over.

10 Take the ends of the band and overlap them to make a circle. Place a small piece of sour apple linen tape on the overlapping ends to hold the circle in place.

17. Daisy Ring

Materials

» Yellow duct tape
» Green duct tape
» Small piece of cardstock

Additional tools

» Pen
» Pencil
» Parchment paper
» Circles stencil

1 Make a petal stencil by drawing a petal shape on a piece of cardstock. The petal should be 1 in. (2.5 cm) high and ½ in. (1.25 cm) wide. Cut out the petal from the cardstock.

2 On a 3 in. (7.5 cm) double-sided strip of yellow tape trace the petal eight times. Cut out the petals.

3 On a piece of parchment paper trace two ¾ in. (1.9 cm) diameter circles. Place a piece of green tape on the paper so it covers the circles. Flip it over so you can see the circles through the paper. Cut out the circles.

4 Remove the paper from one of the circles. Place it on the worktable with the sticky side facing up. Take four of the petals and place each of them halfway on the circle at 0, 90, 180, and 270 degrees.

1

2

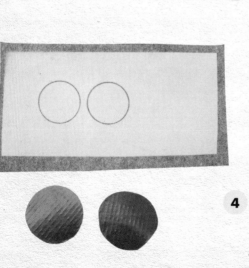

3

4

5

6

7

9

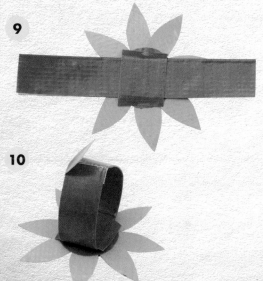

10

5 Take the remaining four petals and place each of them halfway on the circle between the first four petals.

6 Remove the paper from the remaining circle. Place it in the center of the petals. This is the daisy.

7 Cut a 3 in. (7.5 cm) strip of green tape. Cut it in half lengthwise. Take one of the half strips and fold it lengthwise so it is ¼ in. (6 mm) wide. This is the band.

8 Place the daisy on the worktable. Place the band in the horizontal position on top of the daisy.

9 Take a piece of green tape and use to adhere the band to the back of the daisy. Trim off any excess tape around the daisy and band so it is not visible once it is flipped over.

10 Take the ends of the band and overlap them to make a circle. Place a small piece of green tape on the overlapping ends to hold the circle in place.

CHAPTER 2:

Head & Neck Gear

I was once shopping in New York City with my daughter Masana, my sister Elle, and her daughter Katie when I spotted a store with head forms displaying hats and such. Immediately I was like a moth drawn to a light and headed straight for the front door.

Between the cloche hats and the plumed headbands, I was in heaven. The colors, the fringes, the feathers, the rhinestones! My laser-focus on each and every item forced us to spend an hour in there. I wanted EVERYTHING. But my sensible daughter shook her head and pried an expensive peacock headdress out of my hands, and I left empty-handed.

In this section I tried to recreate some of the beautiful hats, headbands, and barrettes from that store. It's been a few years since I've seen those beauties in person, but they linger in my imagination and inspire me to keep on crafting.

Clasps and jump rings for necklaces can be upcycled from old broken necklaces, or you can buy them from a local craft supply shop. A head form or wig stand is useful when creating hats, but a small blow-up ball works too.

18. Double Strip Headband

1 Cut a 24 in. (61 cm) strip of purple and white polka dot tape. Fold it vertically to create a double-sided 12 in. (30.5 cm) strip.

2 Cut two ½ in. (1.25 cm) wide strips and discard the rest.

3 Take the two strips and connect them to form a "V". Take a 1 in. (2.5 cm) wide strip of black tape and wrap it around the joined ends to secure.

4 Join the other ends of the strips with another 1 in. (2.5 cm) wide strip of black tape.

5 Cut a 12 in. (30.5 cm) strip of black tape. Cut in half lengthwise.

6 Fold each half strip into thirds. These are the bands.

7 Attach each band to the ends of the polka dot strips with small pieces of black tape.

19. Gold Leaf Headband

1 Cut a 24 in. (61 cm) strip of gold tape. Cut it in half lengthwise. Set one of the half strips aside.

2 Fold the remaining half strip into thirds. This is the band.

3 On the cardstock draw a leaf 1 in. (2.5 cm) high by 1 in. (2.5 cm) wide. Cut out the leaf. This is the leaf stencil.

4 Cut a 12 in. (30.5 cm) strip of tape. Fold it over vertically to create a double-sided 6 in. (15 cm) strip.

5 Take the leaf stencil and trace it onto the double-sided strip 12 times. Cut out each leaf.

6 Fasten the band onto your worktable lengthwise with small pieces of tape at opposite ends. Starting 6 ½ in. (16.5 cm) from the left-hand end, stick a leaf on alternating sides of the band 1 in. (2.5 cm) apart.

7 Cut the remaining half strip from step 1 vertically in half. Place one of the strips on the worktable lengthwise with the sticky side facing up. Place one end of the headband on top of the strip, 1 in. (2.5 cm) from the right-hand edge and lined up with the bottom edge. Fold the strip in thirds around the headband, making an extension. Repeat on the other end of the headband with the remaining strip.

5

6

7

20. Oval Double-Row Headband

Materials

» Leopard print duct tape
» ½ in. (1.25 cm) wide black elastic band, 10 in. (25 cm) long

Additional tools

» Oval double-row pattern: www.richelafabianmorgan.com
» Pen

1 Cut a 24 in. (61 cm) strip of tape. Fold it over vertically to create a 12 in. (30.5 cm) double-sided strip.

2 Cut out the oval double-row pattern from paper.

1

2

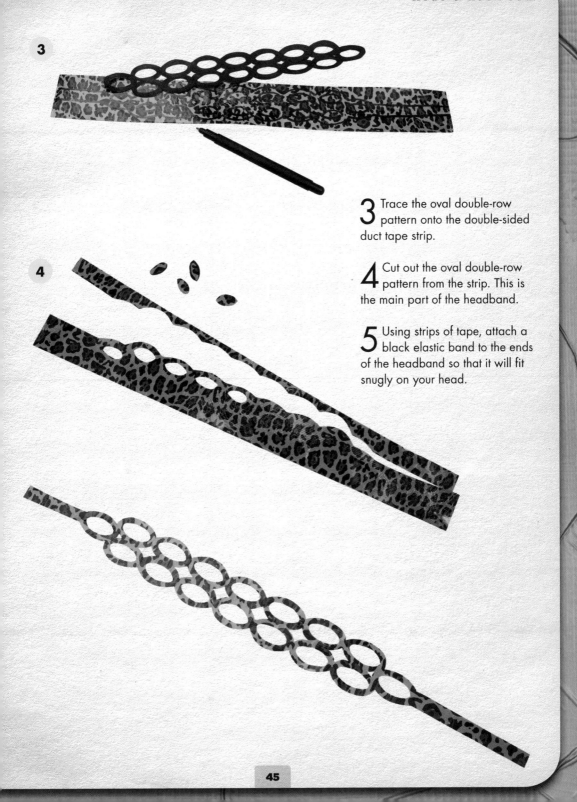

3

3 Trace the oval double-row pattern onto the double-sided duct tape strip.

4

4 Cut out the oval double-row pattern from the strip. This is the main part of the headband.

5 Using strips of tape, attach a black elastic band to the ends of the headband so that it will fit snugly on your head.

21. Feather Bow Hair Clip

Materials

» Red duct tape
» Leopard print duct tape
» Black duct tape
» Velcro® tab

1 Cut a 10 in. (25 cm) strip of red tape. Fold it over vertically to create a 5 in. (12.5 cm) double-sided strip. Cut the strip vertically in half to make two 2 ½ in. (6.5 cm) wide pieces.

2 Fold each piece in half lengthwise and cut a heart shape.

3 Holding each piece in half, cut slits at a 45-degree angle toward the folded edge. Unfold. These are the two red feathers.

4 Cut an 8 in. (20 cm) strip of leopard print tape. Fold it over vertically to create a 4 in. (10 cm) double-sided strip. Cut the strip in half vertically to make two 2 in. (5 cm) wide pieces.

5 Fold each piece in half lengthwise and cut a heart shape.

6 Holding each piece in half, cut slits at a 45-degree angle toward the folded edge. Unfold. These are the two leopard print feathers.

7 Cut a 5 ½ in. (14 cm) strip of red tape. Cut lengthwise into four equal strips.

8 Place the red feathers sideways and next to each other on the worktable, the stems overlapping in the center. Take one of the red tape strips and begin wrapping it around the stems, connecting the feathers together.

9 After wrapping the strip around once, place the leopard print feathers on top. Be sure the feather stems overlap in the center directly on top of the red feathers. Wrap the red strip around the stems. Add another red strip around the stems if needed. This is the feather bow.

10 Cut a 24 in. (61 cm) strip of black tape. Fold it in half lengthwise. This is the band.

11 Place the feather bow on the center of the band lengthwise. Wrap a red strip around the center of the bow and band to join together.

12 Take the remaining red strip and cut a ⅛ in. (3 mm) wide strip. Place the strip across the horizontal middle of the feather bow. This should extend past the outer edges of the bow to the band, holding it down. Trim off the excess.

13 Cut a ⅛ in. (3 mm) high by 2 in. (5 cm) wide strip of leopard tape. Wrap it vertically around the middle of the feather bow.

14 Add a Velcro® tab on the ends of the band.

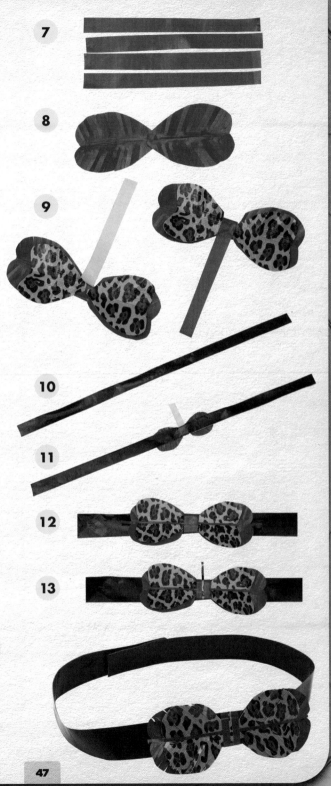

22. Giant Bow Headband

Materials

» Flower wallpaper print duct tape
» Green duct tape
» Velcro® tab

1 Using the flower wallpaper tape, make a double-sided fabric measuring 16 in. (41 cm) wide by 5 in. (12.5 cm) high. Square up the sides.

2 Measure 4 in. (10 cm) inward from the left-hand edge and vertically fold the fabric. Repeat on the right edge.

3 Cut a 10 in. (25 cm) strip of green tape. Cut it in half lengthwise. Set one of the half strips aside.

4 Cut the remaining strip in half vertically. Use one of the strips to connect the edges of the fabric together at the vertical center.

1

2

3

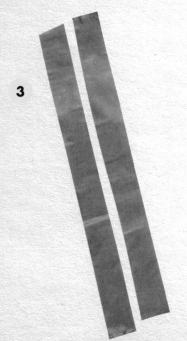

4

5

5 Fold the fabric horizontally to form an accordion with six equal sections.

6 Use the second strip from step 4 and wrap it around the center, holding the accordion fold. Pull out the outer edge folds to form a bow.

7 Cut a 24 in. (61 cm) strip of green tape. Fold it in half lengthwise. This is the band.

8 Wrap the remaining strip from step 3 around the center of the bow and the middle of the band.

9 Attach a Velcro® tab to the ends of the band.

6

7

8

23. Butterfly Hair Clip

1 Using the yellow tape, make a double-sided fabric measuring 2 in. (5 cm) wide by 5 in. (12.5 cm) high.

2 Cut out the butterfly pattern to make three stencils; the upper wing, the lower wing, and the body/antennae.

3 Trace the upper and lower wings twice onto the yellow fabric. Cut out pieces.

4 Cut a 10 in. (25 cm) strip of zebra print tape. Fold in half vertically to make a 5 in. (12.5 cm) double-sided strip.

5 Trace the body/antennae onto the zebra strip and cut out the piece.

Materials

» Yellow duct tape
» Pink and black zebra print duct tape
» Hair clip

Additional tools

» Butterfly pattern: www.richelafabianmorgan.com

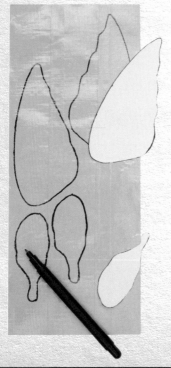

6

6 Assemble the wings on the worktable. Hold the pieces together with small strips of yellow tape. Place the wings next to each other making sure there is at least ¼ in. (6 mm) vertical gap between them.

7 Place a strip of yellow tape in the gap to connect the wings. Flip the wings over. The tape in the center should have the sticky surface exposed.

8 Place the body/antennae between the wings. The tape in the center should hold it in place. This is the butterfly.

9 Flip the butterfly over. Place the reverse side of the hair clip vertically at the center of the butterfly and attach it with small strips of yellow tape.

7

8

9

24. Feather Hair Clip

Materials

» Blue duct tape
» Black duct tape
» Gold duct tape
» 22 gauge florists wire
» Hair clip

Additional tools

» Wire cutters

1 Cut an 18 in. (46 cm) strip of blue tape. Fold in half vertically to make a 9 in. (23 cm) double-sided strip.

2 Fold the strip in half lengthwise. Create a feather shape by rounding the corners on one end and cutting a stem at the other. Unfold the strip. This is the first feather.

3 Cut a blue tape strip measuring ¼ in. (6 mm) by 8 ½ in. (21.5 cm). Flip over so the sticky side is facing up. Cut a piece of wire measuring 8 ½ in. (21.5 cm) long and place it lengthwise along the middle of the strip.

4 Flip the wired strip over and place it lengthwise along the middle of the feather from step 2.

1

2

3

4

5

5 Refold the feather. Starting at the bottom near the stem, cut slits at a 45-degree angle. Unfold.

6 Using the black tape and the gold tape, repeat steps 1–5 so you have three feathers, one in each of the tape colors.

6

7 Place the feathers on top of each other. Stagger them about 1 in. (2.5 cm) lengthwise. Flip the feathers over and using small pieces of tape, fasten together at the stems.

8 Attach the reverse side of the hair clip to the back of the feathers with small pieces of tape. Trim off excess tape.

7

8

25. Large Flower Hair Clip

Materials

» White duct tape
» Hot pink duct tape
» Hemp cord
» 22 gauge florists wire
» Hair clip

Additional tools

» Large petal pattern: www.richelafabianmorgan.com
» Pen
» Large sewing needle
» Wire cutters

1 Using the white tape, make a double-sided fabric measuring 24 in. (61 cm) wide by 4 in. (10 cm) high. Add a 24 in. (61 cm) strip along the top of the fabric and flip over so the sticky side is facing up.

2 Cut a 24 in. (61 cm) strip of white tape. Cut it in half lengthwise. Discard one of the strips. Place the remaining strip at the top edge of the duct tape fabric.

3 Flip the fabric over. Add another 24 in. (61 cm) strip along the top edge.

4 Flip the fabric over; there should be a vertical double-sided strip on the sticky surface on the top. Fold the top edge down, making the vertical crease directly in the middle of the double-sided strip.

5 Cut out the large petal pattern to create a stencil. Trace five petals onto the fabric, the bottom end of the petal lining up with the top edge of the fabric.

6 Cut out the petals. At the base of each petal there should now be a loop. Thread the needle with an 8 in. (20 cm) piece of hemp cord and push it through the loops, connecting the petals together. Remove the needle and pull the ends of the cord. Tie the ends in a double-knot to create a ¼ in. (6 mm) wide diameter circle. Do NOT trim the ends of the cord.

7 Use small pieces of white tape to hold the petals together on one side of the flower. Flip over the flower.

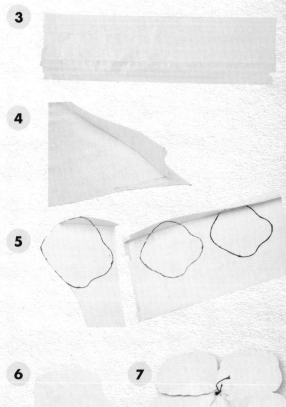

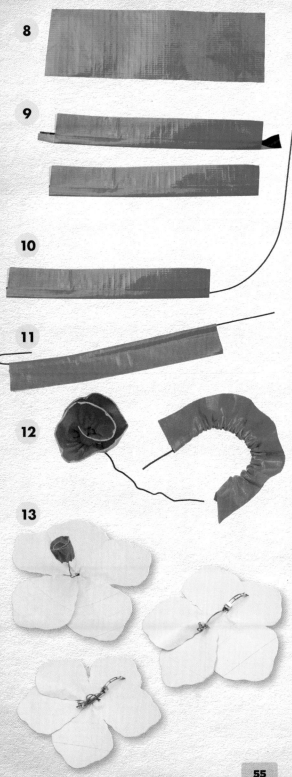

8 Cut a 6 in. (15 cm) strip of pink tape. Flip over so the sticky side is facing up. Using either color, place a 7 in. (18 cm) by ½ in. (1.25 cm) strip of tape lengthwise across the middle of the pink strip.

9 Fold the strip in half lengthwise. Trim off the excess tape at the outer edges.

10 Cut an 8 in. (20 cm) piece of wire. Push it through the loop of the folded pink strip.

11 Bend one end of the wire to hold it in place. Gather the pink strip and push it towards the end with the bent wire to a width of 3 in. (7.5 cm).

12 Twist it around to form a tight spiral. This is the inner flower. Bend the long end of the wire and place it through the middle hole of the larger white flower.

13 Flip the flower over. Tie the wire and the cord ends around the reverse side of the hair clip. Trim any excess wire and cord. Attach the reverse side of the hair clip to the flower with small pieces of white tape.

26. Feather Headdress

Materials

» Gold duct tape
» Brown leather duct tape
» Dark blue duct tape
» White linen duct tape

Additional tools

» Grease pencil

1 Cut a 24 in. (61 cm) strip of gold tape. Cut it lengthwise into four equal ½ in. (1.25 cm) wide strips.

2 Fold each of the strips lengthwise in thirds. These are the headdress bands.

3 Fold strips of brown leather tape over each of the bands, forming double-sided strips measuring 4 ½ in. (11.5 cm) The first band should have six double-sided strips, each band after that should have one less double-sided strip: First band = six, Second band = five, Third band = four, Fourth band = three.

3

4 Fold each of the double-sided strips in half at the end opposite the band and mark with a grease pencil. At this mark, cut off the sides of each strip at an angle, starting at the base near the band. This will form each double-sided strip into a triangle.

5 Cut a 10 in. (25 cm) strip of white linen tape. Divide it into ¼ in. (6 mm) wide pieces.

6 Place a strip of white linen tape lengthwise across each triangle, 1 in. (2.5 cm) from the top. Place a second strip of white tape lengthwise across each triangle, 1 ½ in. (4 cm) from the bottom.

1

2

4

5

6

7 Cut a 5 in. (12.5 cm) strip of blue tape. Divide it into ¼ in. (6 mm) wide pieces. Place one piece lengthwise across each brown triangle, in the middle of the two white linen strips.

8 Trim off any excess blue and white linen tape at the outer edges of each triangle.

9 Cut vertical slits into each triangle ⅛-¼ in. (3-6 mm) apart. These are the feathers.

10 Place the first band (containing six feathers) stripes facing up on the worktable. Place the other bands in number order on top. Vertically stagger them by 1 in. (2.5 cm) and then curve the bands to form an arch.

11 To hold the staggered position, place a 2 in. (5 cm) strip of gold tape on the bands at the sides and fold the tape strips over. This is the feathered headdress.

12 Flip the headdress over. Place small strips of tape on the back of the feathers to hold the arch shape.

13 Cut two 14 in. (35.5 cm) strips of gold tape and place on the worktable lengthwise with the sticky sides facing up.

14 Flip the headdress once more. Place one side of bands on the outer edge of one of the gold tape strips. Fold tape strip over the bands. Then place the other set of bands on the outer edge of the remaining gold tape strip. Fold tape strip over the bands. These are the finished side straps.

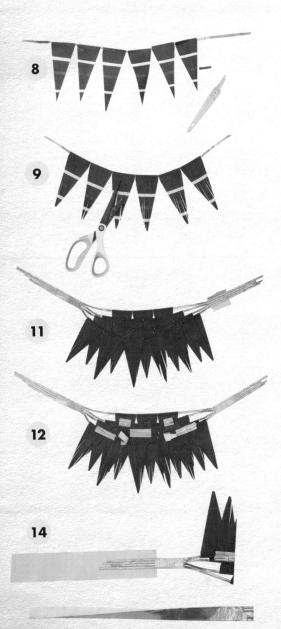

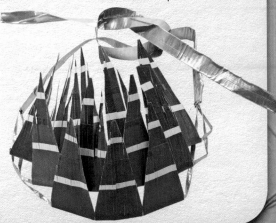

27. Laurel Wreath

Materials

» Grass duct tape
» Paddle wire

Additional tools

» Cardstock
» Grease pencil
» Tape measure
» Wire cutters

1 Using the following leaf pattern, make a leaf stencil out of the cardstock. The laurel leaf should measure 1 5/16 in. (3.3 cm) by 2 7/16 in. (6.2 cm).

2 Make double-sided strips of tape. Trace and cut out 20 laurel leaves.

1

2

58

4

5

3 Measure the circumference of the crown of your head. Cut two sections of wire with that measurement. Curve both wires into two circles and connect the ends with tape.

4 Using small pieces of tape, attach ten leaves to each circle, five leaves per side.

5 Twist the wire circles together to make the wreath.

28. Visor

Materials

» Skateboard duct tape
» Denim duct tape
» 3 in. (7.5 cm) Velcro® strip

Additional tools

» Visor pattern:
www.richelafabianmorgan.com

1 Using the denim tape, make a double-sided layered fabric measuring 10 in. (25 cm) wide by 6 in. (15 cm) high. Trace the visor pattern on the fabric and cut out the piece. This is the visor brim. Set it aside.

2 Cut a 24 in. (61 cm) strip of skateboard tape. Fold in half lengthwise. This is the strap. Set aside.

3 Make a 9 in. (23 cm) double-sided strip using the skateboard tape. This is the visor top. Set aside.

4 Cut a 9 in. (23 cm) strip of skateboard tape. Lay it on the worktable lengthwise with the sticky side facing up. Place the strap lengthwise on the center of the strip. Be sure there are equal lengths of the strap extending past each outer edge of the strip.

1

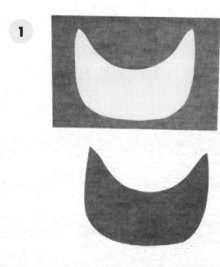

2

3

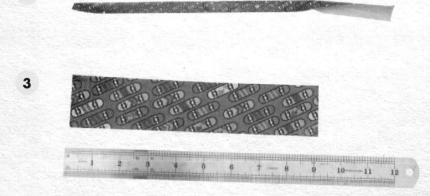

4

5

6

7

5 Place the visor top lengthwise on top of the strip. Be sure to place it squarely on top so the edges line up. Smooth down with your hand.

6 Cut another 9 in. (23 cm) strip of skateboard tape, then cut it in half lengthwise. Discard one of the half strips. Place the remaining half strip lengthwise and halfway across the bottom of the visor top. Flip over. There should be a sticky border at the bottom of the visor top. Cut vertical strips across the sticky border approximately ½ in. (1.25 cm) apart.

7 Line up the bottom edge of the visor top with the inside curve of the visor brim. Press the sticky border against the backside of the brim as you work around the curve.

8 Remove one of the backings from the Velcro® strip. Attach the strip to one of the strap ends. Remove the other backing and attach the remaining strap end to the Velcro® strip.

29. Cloche Hat

Materials

» Yellow duct tape
» White duct tape
» Red duct tape

Additional tools

» ⅛ in. (3 mm) diameter hole punch
» Cloche hat pattern:
  www.richelafabianmorgan.com

1 There are three patterns for the cloche hat: the body, the top, and the brim. The pattern for the body found on the website is only half of it. The other half is the mirror image of it. In order to get the full body pattern, you must vertically connect both pieces at the broken line. The full width of the body pattern is 12 in. (30.5 cm).

2 Using the yellow tape, make a double-sided layered fabric ensuring it is large enough to fit two of the body patterns inside it. Trace the pattern twice onto the fabric and cut out the pieces.

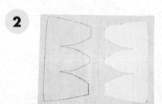

3 Make another yellow double-sided layered fabric ensuring it is large enough to fit two of the brim patterns and one of the top patterns. Trace the brim pattern twice and the top pattern once onto the fabric. Cut out the pieces.

4 Using strips of tape, connect the seams on the two body pieces. Then connect the two pieces together.

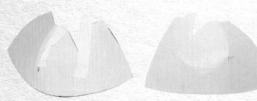

5 Place the top piece inside the body so it covers the small hole at the apex. Secure the top in place with strips of tape.

6 Attach the brim pieces to the bottom edge of the body with strips of tape along the reverse side of the seam. This is the cloche hat.

7

7 Cut a 25 in. (63.5 cm) strip of white tape and place it on the worktable lengthwise with the sticky side facing up. Fold down the top and bottom edge ¼ in. (6 mm). Flip over and wrap around the hat where the brim and body connect. Press down the strip as you wrap it around. This is the hat band.

8

8 Cut three 8 in. (20.5 cm) strips of red tape. Fold each one lengthwise, then pull the bottom edge up ¼ in. (6 mm) below the top edge.

9

9 Roll each folded strip, starting with a tight circle and progressively loosening the spiral. As you roll the strip, pinch the edge with the exposed sticky border. These are flowers.

10

10 Roll a 6 in. (15 cm) strip of red tape around the base of each flower, twisting it into a stem.

11

11 Punch three holes through the band area of the hat. Be sure the holes go all the way through the hat. Push the stem of each flower through the holes. Trim down the stems on the inside of the hat.

30. **Cycling Cap**

Materials

» Pink argyle duct tape
» Emerald tile duct tape
» Bacon duct tape

Additional tools

» Cycling cap patterns:
   www.richelafabianmorgan.com

1 There are three patterns used to make the cycling cap: the side, the top, and the brim.

2 Using the pink argyle tape, make a double-sided layered fabric large enough to fit the top and brim patterns inside. Trace the top and brim patterns onto the fabric and cut out the pieces.

2

3

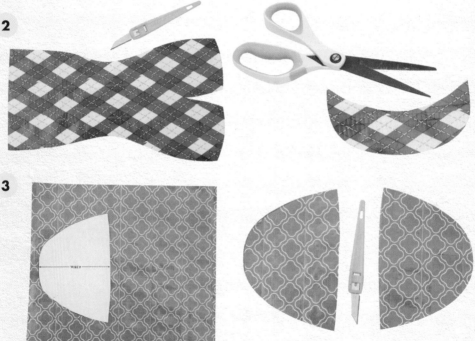

4

3 With the emerald tile tape, make a double-sided layered fabric large enough to fit two of the side patterns inside. Trace the side pattern twice onto the fabric and cut out the pieces.

5

6

4 Use strips of tape to connect the seams on the top piece.

5 Use strips of tape to attach the sides to the top piece. This is the base of the cap.

6 Attach a strip of bacon tape lengthwise and halfway around the bottom edge of the cap. Then fold the strip inward, creating a border.

7 Place a strip of argyle tape lengthwise and halfway across the bottom of the inside curve of the brim. Flip over and cut vertical strips ½ in. (1.25 cm) apart, across the sticky border. Line up the inside curve edge of the brim with the bottom edge of the cap. Be sure it is the front of the cap. Press the sticky border against the inside of the cap as you work around the curve.

7

31. Top Hat

Materials

» Tangerine chevron duct tape
» Black and white gingham duct tape
» White duct tape

Additional tools

» Tape measure

1 Measure the circumference of your head. Using tangerine chevron tape for the outside and white tape for the reverse, make a double-sided layered fabric. The width is the same measurement as your head circumference and the height is 5 ½ in. (14 cm). Square up the sides. With a white strip of tape connect the ends to make an oval. This is the body of the hat.

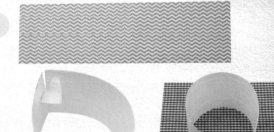

2 With black and white gingham tape and white tape, make a double-sided layered fabric large enough to fit the body plus 3 in. (7.5 cm) all around the perimeter. Place the body in the center of the fabric. Make slight adjustments to ensure it's symmetrical. Trace the body onto the fabric from the outside.

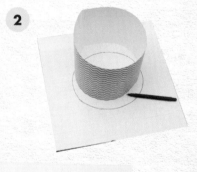

3 Measure and mark 2 in. (5 cm) all around the body, making an outer oval. Cut out the inner oval piece. This is the top. Then cut out the outer oval. This is the hat brim.

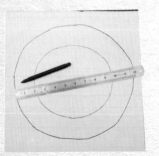
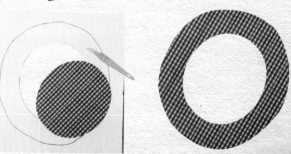

5

4 Cut and place a strip of white tape lengthwise, halfway along the inside of the body's top edge. Cut vertical slits, ½ in. (1.25 cm) apart, into the sticky border of the strip.

5 Carefully attach the top's edge to the body's top edge. Press down the sticky strip along the inside of the top as you work around the oval.

6

6 Place a strip of white tape halfway along the inside of the body's bottom edge, lengthwise. Cut vertical slits, ½ in. (1.25 cm) apart, into the sticky border of the strip.

7 Carefully attach the brim to the body's bottom edge. Press down the sticky strip along the backside of the brim as you work around the oval. This is the hat.

7

32. Easter Hat

Materials

» White duct tape
» Cotton candy duct tape

Additional tools

» Tape measure
» ⅛ in. (3 mm) diameter hole punch

1 Measure the circumference of your head. Then make a double-sided layered fabric using the white tape. The width is the same measurement as your head's circumference. The height is 3 in. (7.5 cm). Square up the sides. With a white strip of tape connect the ends to make an oval. This is the body of the hat.

1

2 Make a double-sided layered fabric using the white tape. It should be large enough to fit the body plus 4 in. (10 cm) around the perimeter. Place the body in the center of the fabric. Make slight adjustments to make sure it's symmetrical. Trace the body onto the fabric from the outside.

2

3 Measure and mark a second oval ½ in. (1.25 cm) larger.

3

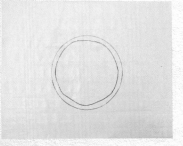

4 From this second oval measure and mark a third oval 3 in. (7.5 cm) larger.

4

5 Cut out the second (middle) oval. This is the hat top. Then cut out the third (outer) oval. This is the hat brim.

5

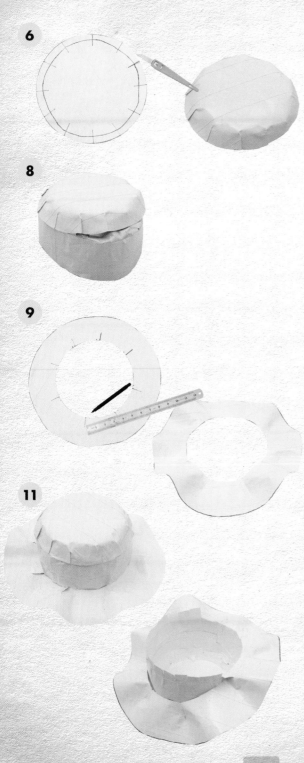

6 Cut 12 slits into the top from the outer edge, each 1 in. (2.5 cm) long and of equal distance to each other. At the start of every slit, overlap the corners ⅜ in. (1 cm) and hold the curve with white tape strips. When you are done, the overall circumference should be the same as the body. Make adjustments if necessary.

7 Place a strip of white tape halfway along the inside top edge of the body, lengthwise. Cut vertical slits, ½ in. (1.25 cm) apart, into the sticky border of the strip.

8 Carefully attach the top's edge to the top edge of the body, pressing down the sticky strip along the inside of the top as you work around the oval.

9 Cut eight 1 in. (2.5 cm) slits into the inner edge of the brim, equal distance to each other. At the start of every slit, overlap the corners ⅜ in. (1 cm) and hold the curve with white tape strips. When done, the overall circumference should be the same as the body. Make adjustments if necessary.

10 Place a strip of white tape halfway along the inside of the body's bottom edge, lengthwise. Cut vertical slits, 1 in. (2.5 cm) apart, into the sticky border of the strip.

11 Carefully attach the brim's inner to the body's bottom edge. Press down the sticky strip along the reverse side of the brim as you work around the oval. This is the hat.

12

12 Cut a strip of cotton candy tape the same length as the circumference of your head. Place on the worktable lengthwise with the sticky side facing up. Fold the top and bottom edges inwards ¼ in. (6 mm). Flip over and place the strip around the hat, close to the brim. This is the band.

13 Cut two 12 in. (30.5 cm) strips of cotton candy tape. Place one strip lengthwise on the worktable with sticky side facing up. Fold the bottom edge inwards ¼–½ in. (3–6 mm). Place the second strip, sticky side down, on top of the first strip so the bottom edge slightly overlaps the folded border. Flip over. Place vertically on the worktable and roll the fabric. Start with a tight circle and progressively loosen the spiral. As you roll the fabric, pinch the edge with the exposed sticky border. This is a flower.

14 Repeat step 13 to make the second flower.

13

15 Poke two holes through the band area of the hat. Be sure the holes go all the way through the hat. Push the stem of each flower through the holes. Trim down the stems on the inside of the hat.

14

15

Materials

» Black duct tape
» Blue chevron duct tape
» Two jump rings
» Clasp

Additional tools

» Flat nose pliers

33. Feathered Pendant Necklace

1 Cut a 24 in. (61 cm) strip of black tape. Cut off a ½ in. (1.25 cm) wide strip. Fold the strip lengthwise in thirds. This is the necklace rope. Secure it to the worktable lengthwise by placing strips of tape on the ends. Set the extra tape aside.

2 Cut a 4 in. (10 cm) strip of blue chevron tape and fold it over the center of the rope. Cut two 3 ½ in. (9 cm) strips of blue chevron tape and fold them over the rope to the left and right of the middle folded chevron strip.

3 Cut the folded strips into triangles.

4 Cut vertical slits ⅛ in. (3 mm) apart, into each triangle.

5 Using the extra tape from step 1, cut small pieces and use them to attach the jump rings to the ends of the rope.

6 Attach the clasp to one of the jump rings.

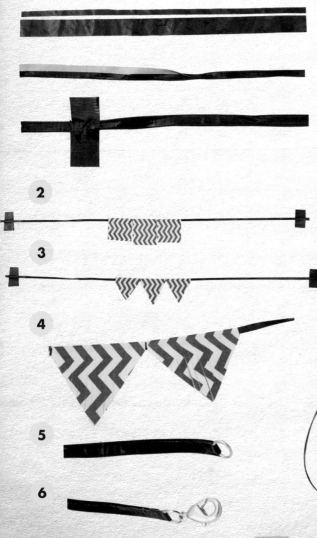

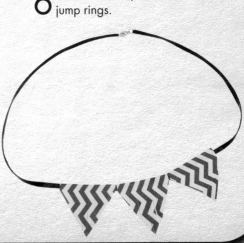

34. Bow Tie

Materials

» Comic book duct tape
» Red duct tape
» Velcro® tab

1 Using the comic book tape, make a double-sided fabric measuring 11 in. (28 cm) wide by 3 ½ in. (9 cm) high. Square up the sides.

2 Vertically fold the fabric 2 ¼ in. (6 cm) in from the left edge. Repeat on the right edge.

3 Cut an 8 in. (20 cm) strip of red tape. Cut it in half lengthwise. Set one of the half strips aside.

4 Cut the remaining strip in half vertically. Use one of the strips to connect the edges of the fabric together at the vertical center.

5 Fold the fabric horizontally to form an accordion with six equal sections.

1

2

4

5

6 Use the second strip from step 4 and wrap it around the center, holding the accordion fold. Pull out the folds at the outer edges to form a bow.

7 Cut a 24 in. (61 cm) strip of red tape. Fold it in thirds lengthwise. This is the band.

8 Wrap the remaining strip from step 3 around the center of the bow and the middle of the band.

9 Attach a Velcro® tab to the ends of the band.

35. Piano Skinny Tie

Materials

» White duct tape
» Black duct tape

1 Using the white tape, make a 24 in. (61 cm) double-sided strip.

1

2 Cut a 28 in. (71 cm) white tape strip. Fold it in half lengthwise.

2

3 Connect one end of the double-sided strip with one end of the folded white tape. Flip over and place a second piece of white tape where the strips meet. This is the full length of the tie.

3

4 Trim excess tape at joining point of strips at 45-degree angles.

4

5 At the wider end of the tie, fold the edge in half. Along the unfolded side measure 1 ½ in. (4 cm) in from the end and mark it. Starting at that mark, cut off the corners at an angle, ending your cut at the folded corner. Unfold. This is the front end of the tie.

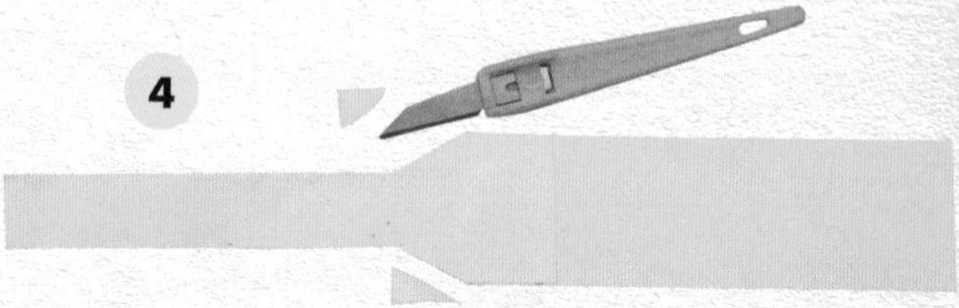

5

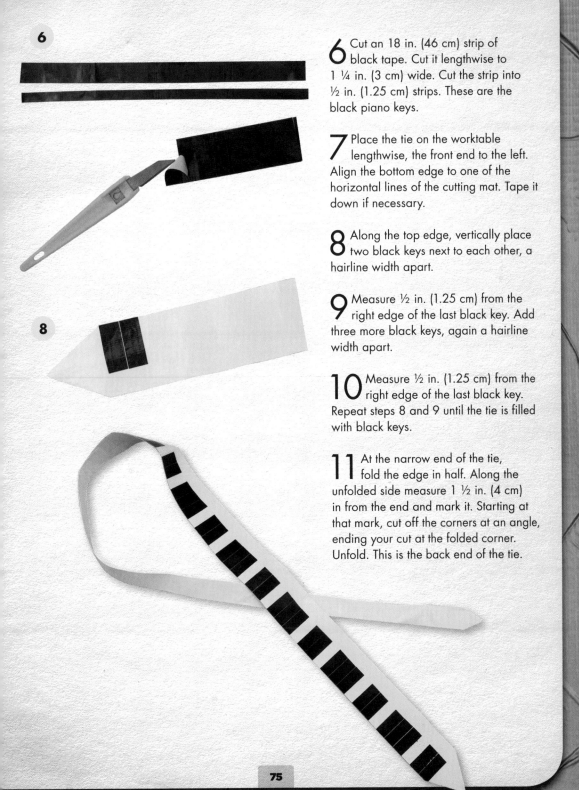

6 Cut an 18 in. (46 cm) strip of black tape. Cut it lengthwise to 1 ¼ in. (3 cm) wide. Cut the strip into ½ in. (1.25 cm) strips. These are the black piano keys.

7 Place the tie on the worktable lengthwise, the front end to the left. Align the bottom edge to one of the horizontal lines of the cutting mat. Tape it down if necessary.

8 Along the top edge, vertically place two black keys next to each other, a hairline width apart.

9 Measure ½ in. (1.25 cm) from the right edge of the last black key. Add three more black keys, again a hairline width apart.

10 Measure ½ in. (1.25 cm) from the right edge of the last black key. Repeat steps 8 and 9 until the tie is filled with black keys.

11 At the narrow end of the tie, fold the edge in half. Along the unfolded side measure 1 ½ in. (4 cm) in from the end and mark it. Starting at that mark, cut off the corners at an angle, ending your cut at the folded corner. Unfold. This is the back end of the tie.

36. Ascot Tie

1 Using the yellow tape, make two double-sided layered fabrics measuring 8 in. (20 cm) wide by 5 in. (12.5 cm) high.

2 Using the yellow tape, make a 17 in. (43 cm) double-sided strip.

3 Cut a 3 in. (7.5 cm) strip of leopard tape and place it lengthwise on the worktable with the sticky side facing up. Place one end of the yellow double-sided strip vertically on the top half of the leopard tape.

4 Take one of the yellow fabrics and position it so the 5 in. (12.5 cm) sides are at the top and bottom edges. Fold the top edge accordion style three times. Place that folded edge on top of the leopard tape directly below the double-sided strip. Fold the bottom edge accordion-style as well and line up the outer left and right edges of the fabric with the outer left and right edges of the double-sided yellow strip.

Materials

» Yellow duct tape
» Leopard print duct tape

Additional tools

» Parchment paper
» Pencil

1

2

3

4

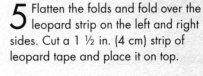

5

5 Flatten the folds and fold over the leopard strip on the left and right sides. Cut a 1 ½ in. (4 cm) strip of leopard tape and place it on top.

6 Repeat steps 3–5, using the remaining end of the double-sided strip and second yellow duct tape fabric.

7 Fold the bottom end of each fabric vertically in half. Round the corners with scissors. This is the finished ascot tie.

7

8 Draw a block letter on the parchment paper and cover it with a piece of leopard tape. Flip the paper over. You should be able to see the letter but in reverse. Using a pair of well-oiled scissors, cut out the letter.

9 Remove the paper from the back of the letter and place it on the ascot tie.

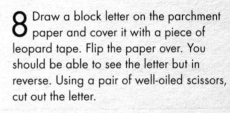

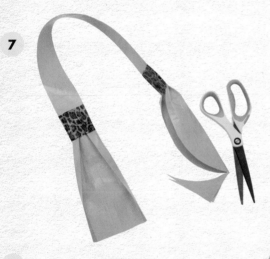

8

37. Bolo Tie

1 Cut a 24 in. (61 cm) strip of black tape. Cut the strip down into a long isosceles triangle, with a 1 in. (2.5 cm) base. Discard the rest of the tape.

2 Place the strip on the worktable with the sticky surface facing up. Fold the base edge in ¼ in. (6 mm).

3 Rub oil on the pencil. Place it lengthwise at the base of the black tape strip and begin rolling the tape around the pencil to make a large bead. Be sure to roll straight up so the apex at the top of the strip eventually finishes in the center of the bead. Push the bead off the pencil and set aside.

Materials

» Black duct tape
» Pink argyle duct tape

Additional tools

» Pencil with a rounded cylinder
» Oil

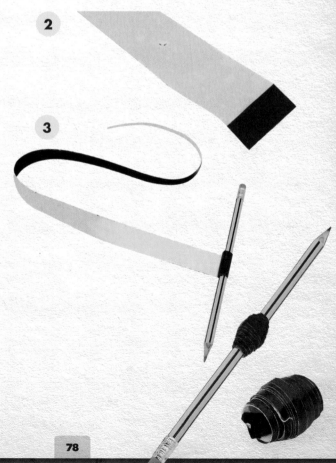

1

2

3

4

5

7

4 Cut a 20 in. (51 cm) strip of pink argyle tape. Cut it in half lengthwise. Discard one of the half strips. Cut the remaining strip in half lengthwise again.

5 Fold each of the strips into thirds to form ropes. Join them together with a small piece of argyle tape to form one 40 in. (102 cm) rope.

6 Fold the rope in half. Push the folded end through the bead.

7 Tie knots at the ends of the rope.

38. Wide Necktie

Materials

» Emerald tile duct tape
» Silver metallic duct tape

Additional tools

» Parchment paper

1 Cut a piece of parchment paper 2 ½ in. (6.5 cm) wide and place horizontally on your worktable.

2 Cut six 5 in. (12.5 cm) strips of emerald tile tape. Place these on the worktable, sticky sides facing up, and fold the bottom edge of each piece up ¼ in. (6 mm).

3 Starting on the left side of the parchment paper, place the folded strips at a 45-degree angle, layering them to overlap ¼ in. (6 mm). The folded edges of the strips should be on the left.

4 Cut a 5 in. (12.5 cm) silver metallic strip of tape and fold the bottom edge up ¼ in. (6 mm). Add it to the layered tape strips on the parchment paper.

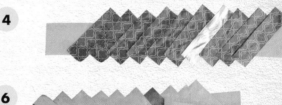

5 Cut three more 5 in. (12.5 cm). strips of emerald tile tape and fold the bottom edges up ¼ in. (6 mm). Add these to the layered tape strips on the parchment paper.

6 Flip over the layered strips and carefully remove the parchment paper. Cover with two strips of silver metallic tape.

7 Flip over and trim down to 3 ½ in. (9 cm) wide.

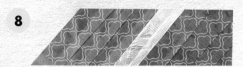

8 The left edge should be angled. Fold in half lengthwise so the folded edge is along the bottom. Trim the bottom layer so it matches the top layer. Unfold. The left edge should now be a sideways "V". This is the front part of the necktie.

9 Along the right edge add three 5 in. (12.5 cm) emerald tile strips of tape at a 45-degree angle, overlapping at the edges by ¼ in. (6 mm). Do not fold the edges. Flip it over so the sticky side is facing up.

10 Make a 28 in. (71 cm) double-sided strip, emerald tile on one side and silver on the other. This is the back part of the necktie. Hold it so the silver side is facing up. Attach one end to the front part of necktie by placing it on top of the sticky side. Cover over the sticky surface with strips of silver tape.

11 Using a craft knife and metal ruler, trim off the excess tape on the sides.

39. Multi-Circle Necklace

Materials

» Candy cane stripe duct tape
» Clasp
» Extra large metal jump ring
» Two jump rings at least ¼ in. (6 mm) diameter

Additional tools

» Circles stencil
» Flat nose pliers

1 Make two 9 in. (23 cm) double-sided strips. Trace seven 1 ½ in. (4 cm) diameter circles, six 1 in. (2.5 cm) diameter circles and 14 circles with a ¾ in. (2 cm) diameter.

2 Inside the 1 ½ in. (4 cm) circles, draw a 1 in. (2.5 cm) diameter circle. Inside the 1 in. (2.5 cm) circles, draw a ⅞ in. (2.25 cm) diameter circle. Inside the ¾ in. (2 cm) circles, draw a ⅝ in. (1.7 cm) diameter circle.

3 Cut out the circles, both the outer and inner, to create rings.

4 The smallest set of rings are the duct tape jump rings. Cut a slit into each of them.

5 Use the duct tape jump rings to connect the large and medium size rings.

2

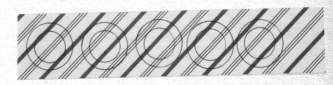

4

5

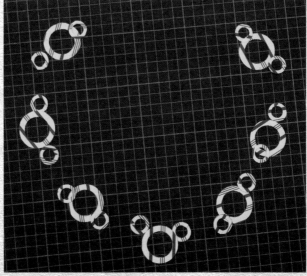

6 Cut small pieces of tape. Use them to close up the slits on the duct tape jump rings. Trim off any excess tape. This is the necklace chain.

7 Attach one of the smaller metal jump rings to one end of the necklace. Add the clasp.

8 Attach the larger metal jump ring to the small duct tape jump ring at the opposite end of the necklace. Then add the smaller jump ring.

6

7

8

40. Pendant Necklace

1 Using the Brazilian rosewood tape, make a double-sided fabric measuring 3 in. (7.5 cm) square. Trace a 2 ¼ in. (6 cm) diameter circle and cut it out.

2 Using the gold tape, make a 2 in. (5 cm) double-sided strip. Trace a 1 ¼ in. (3 cm) diameter circle and cut it out.

3 Using the orange chevron tape, make a 2 ½ in. (6.5 cm) double-sided strip. Trace a 1 ¾ in. (4.5 cm) diameter circle and a ¾ in. (2 cm) diameter circle. Cut both circles out.

4 Punch a hole ⅛ in. (3 mm) from the edge of each of the four circles.

5 Cut a 24 in. (61 cm) strip of gold tape. Then cut off a ½ in. (1.25 cm) wide strip. Fold the strip in thirds lengthwise. This is the necklace rope. Set the extra tape aside.

Materials

» Brazilian rosewood duct tape
» Gold duct tape
» Orange chevron duct tape
» Two jump rings
» Clasp

Additional tools

» Circles stencil
» ¼ in. (6 mm) diameter hole punch
» Flat nose pliers

4

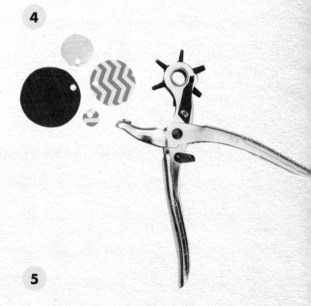

5

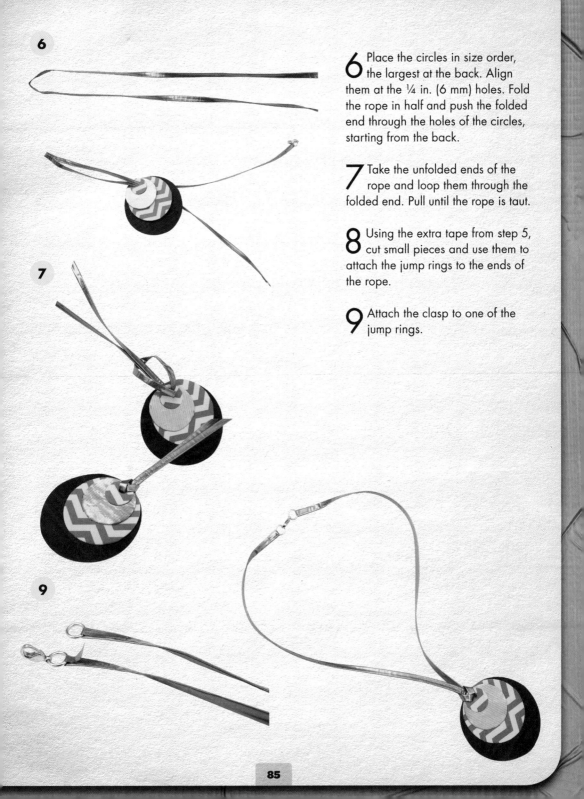

6 Place the circles in size order, the largest at the back. Align them at the ¼ in. (6 mm) holes. Fold the rope in half and push the folded end through the holes of the circles, starting from the back.

7 Take the unfolded ends of the rope and loop them through the folded end. Pull until the rope is taut.

8 Using the extra tape from step 5, cut small pieces and use them to attach the jump rings to the ends of the rope.

9 Attach the clasp to one of the jump rings.

CHAPTER 3

Beautiful Belts

When I told my sister Liza that it was possible to make a belt using duct tape, she responded, "Of course!" Immediately I became skeptical of her quick admission. Liza is hard to impress. So I felt that there was more behind her answer.

Carefully, I asked, "You do?" Liza added, "It's duct tape. You just roll it around your waist and—voila!—you have a belt!" This was accompanied by some equally ridiculous hand gestures, but I'll spare you the details. I wound up laughing with her—and determined to give her something she could see and believe in.

For some belts, a double-sided strip is the base for its construction. You can it make different widths, adding stripes or cutting shapes, then add a buckle. You can also make chain belts, pleated belts, and twisted belts. Just like a necklace or bracelet, you need to cut pieces out of a double-sided strip or fabric and link them together. Buckles can be hard to come by, so either upcycle one or try a local or online craft store. Be sure to measure the width of your belt so you don't purchase the wrong size.

Materials

» Blue surf flower duct tape
» Black duct tape
» 3 in. (7.5 cm) wide tongueless round center bar belt buckle

41. Fabric Belt

1 Using blue surf flower tape, make a 40 in. (102 cm) wide by 3 in. (7.5 cm) high double-sided fabric.

2 Place a 40 in. (102 cm) strip of black tape lengthwise down the middle of the fabric. Square up the sides. This is the main part of the belt.

3 On one end of the belt place a strip of black tape vertically ½ in. (1.25 cm) in from the edge. Flip over and cover the strip with a second strip of black tape.

4 Fold the belt end in half. Using scissors, round off the corners.

5 Weave the opposite end of the belt through the buckle. Secure the end to the reverse of the belt with a piece of blue surf flower tape.

1
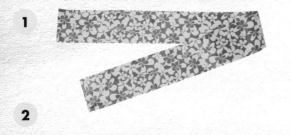

2

3

4

5

42. Rainbow Shape Belt

Materials

» Skateboard duct tape
» Black duct tape
» Metal key chain clip

Additional tools

» Rainbow belt pattern:
  www.richelamorgan.com
» ⅛ in. (3 mm) hole punch

1 Using skateboard tape for the front side and black for the reverse, make a 25 in. (64 cm) wide by 6 in. (15 cm) high double-sided fabric.

2 Fold fabric in half vertically. Place the rainbow pattern on top, lining up the wider end with the folded edge of the fabric. Trace the pattern and remove.

3 Carefully cut out the shape of the rainbow taking care to cut through both layers. This is the main part of the belt. Unfold and discard the excess fabric.

4

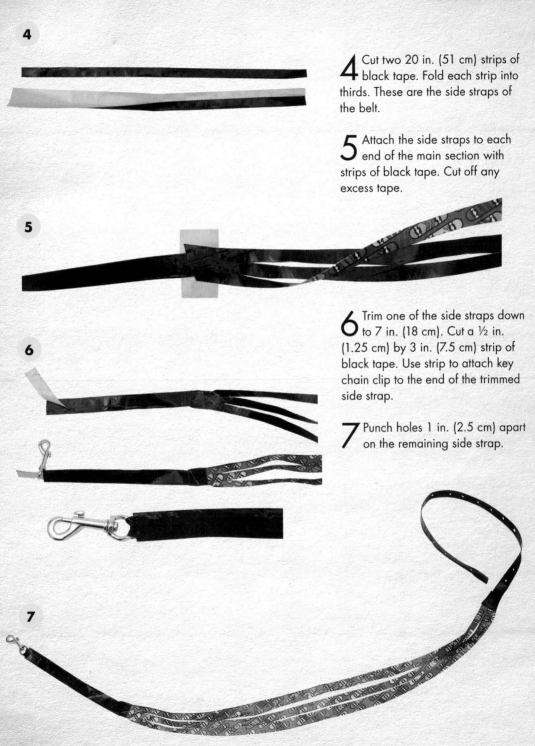

4 Cut two 20 in. (51 cm) strips of black tape. Fold each strip into thirds. These are the side straps of the belt.

5 Attach the side straps to each end of the main section with strips of black tape. Cut off any excess tape.

5

6 Trim one of the side straps down to 7 in. (18 cm). Cut a ½ in. (1.25 cm) by 3 in. (7.5 cm) strip of black tape. Use strip to attach key chain clip to the end of the trimmed side strap.

6

7 Punch holes 1 in. (2.5 cm) apart on the remaining side strap.

7

43. Two-Tone Belt

Materials

- » Brown leather-look duct tape
- » White linen duct tape
- » 2 in. (5 cm) wide center bar belt buckle

Additional tools

- » Circles stencil
- » ⅛ in. (3 mm) hole punch

1 Using brown leather-look tape, make a 40 in. (102 cm) double-sided strip.

2 Cut a 40 in. (102 cm) strip of white linen tape. Trim it down to 1½ in. (4 cm) wide.

3 Place the white strip lengthwise down the middle of the brown double-sided strip.

4 Starting 10 in. (25 cm) from the left-hand edge, measure and mark 5 in. (13 cm) increments along the strip.

1

2

3

4

5

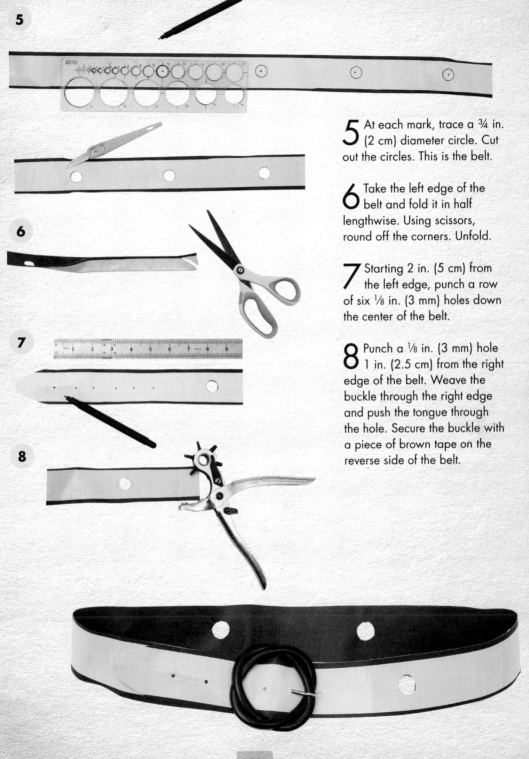

5 At each mark, trace a ¾ in. (2 cm) diameter circle. Cut out the circles. This is the belt.

6 Take the left edge of the belt and fold it in half lengthwise. Using scissors, round off the corners. Unfold.

7 Starting 2 in. (5 cm) from the left edge, punch a row of six ⅛ in. (3 mm) holes down the center of the belt.

8 Punch a ⅛ in. (3 mm) hole 1 in. (2.5 cm) from the right edge of the belt. Weave the buckle through the right edge and push the tongue through the hole. Secure the buckle with a piece of brown tape on the reverse side of the belt.

6

7

8

44. Striped Belt

1 Cut a 40 in. (102 cm) strip of merlot
tape. Fold in half lengthwise. This is
the main belt.

2 Cut at least six ½ in. (1.25 cm) wide
strips in each of the remaining colors.

3 Starting 6 in. (15 cm) from one end of
the belt, place five strips, one of each
color, vertically across the width. Leave
½ in. (1.25 cm) space and add another
group of five strips, one of each color.
Continue adding groups of five strips,
½ in. (1.25 cm) apart, until 3 in. (7.5 cm)
remains at the end of the belt.

4 Flip the belt over and fold the duct tape
strips down.

Materials

» Merlot duct tape
» Dark blue duct tape
» Red duct tape
» Gold duct tape
» Pink duct tape
» Green duct tape
» 1 in. (2.5 cm) wide center
bar belt buckle

Additional tools

» ⅛ in. (3 mm) hole punch

1

2

3

4

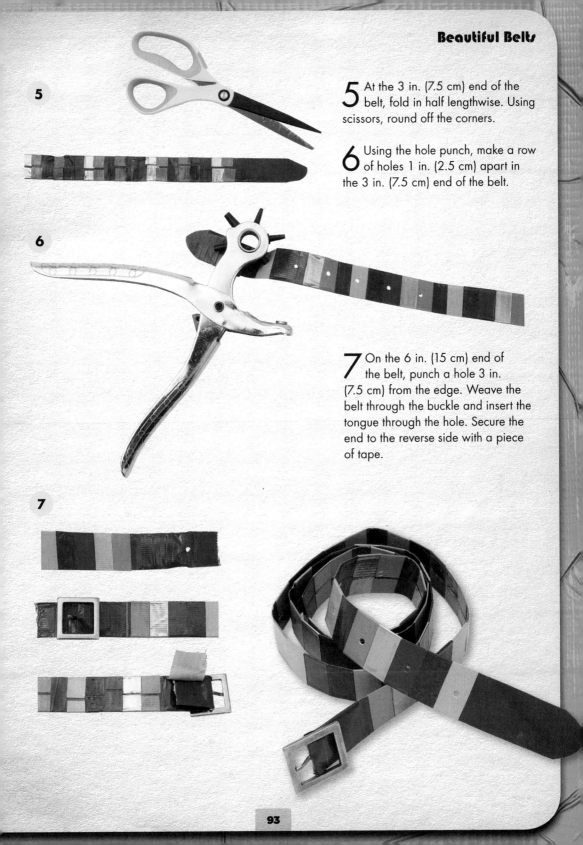

5 At the 3 in. (7.5 cm) end of the belt, fold in half lengthwise. Using scissors, round off the corners.

6 Using the hole punch, make a row of holes 1 in. (2.5 cm) apart in the 3 in. (7.5 cm) end of the belt.

7 On the 6 in. (15 cm) end of the belt, punch a hole 3 in. (7.5 cm) from the edge. Weave the belt through the buckle and insert the tongue through the hole. Secure the end to the reverse side with a piece of tape.

45. Twisted Belt

Materials

» Pink zebra print duct tape
» Black duct tape
» 1 ½ in. (4 cm) wide center bar belt buckle

Additional tools

» ⅛ in. (3 mm) hole punch

1 Cut two 40 in. (102 cm) strips of pink zebra tape. Fold both of them into thirds.

2 Cut seven ½ in. (1.25 cm) wide strips of black tape. Set aside.

1

3 Place the folded strips lengthwise on the worktable. Line up the left edges and hold them down with a piece of tape. Every 5 in. (12.5 cm) cross the strips over. Hold the strips together by wrapping a ½ in. (1.25 cm) wide strip of black tape at each 5 in. (12.5 cm) intersection.

2

3

4

4 Remove the piece of tape holding down one end of the belt. Cut two 2 ½ in. (6.5 cm) strips of black tape. With the folded strips lying flat and close together, wrap one strip around each end of the belt.

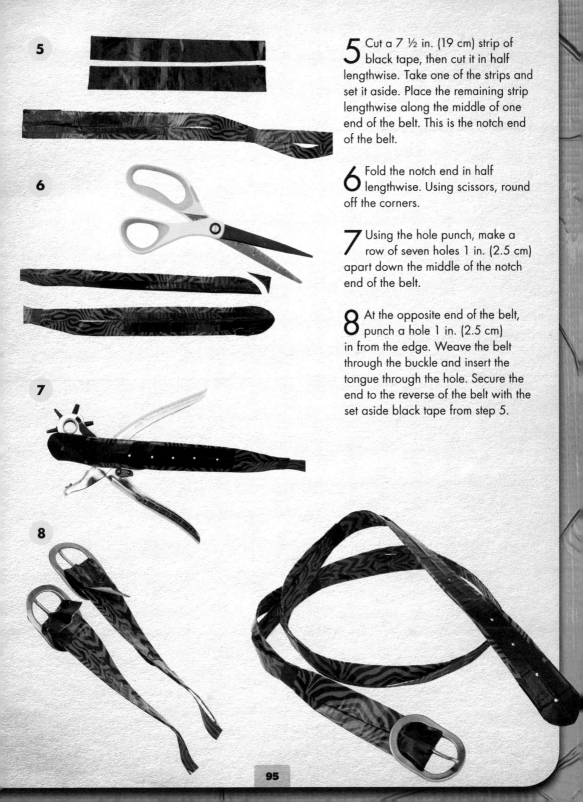

5 Cut a 7 ½ in. (19 cm) strip of black tape, then cut it in half lengthwise. Take one of the strips and set it aside. Place the remaining strip lengthwise along the middle of one end of the belt. This is the notch end of the belt.

6 Fold the notch end in half lengthwise. Using scissors, round off the corners.

7 Using the hole punch, make a row of seven holes 1 in. (2.5 cm) apart down the middle of the notch end of the belt.

8 At the opposite end of the belt, punch a hole 1 in. (2.5 cm) in from the edge. Weave the belt through the buckle and insert the tongue through the hole. Secure the end to the reverse of the belt with the set aside black tape from step 5.

46. Bone Chain Belt

Materials

» Tangerine chevron duct tape
» Blue paisley duct tape
» Black duct tape
» Metal key chain clip

Additional tools

» 2 ⅛ in. (5.5 cm) wide bone chain stencil
» ¼ in. (6 mm) hole punch

1 Using tangerine chevron tape on one side and blue paisley tape on the other, make a 35 in. (89 cm) long double-sided strip.

2 Make a bone chain stencil by tracing the following pattern. On the tangerine chevron side, trace the stencil 20 times or more for a longer belt.

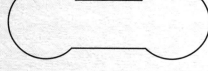

3 Using scissors, cut out each bone.

4 With the hole punch, make a ¼ in. (6 mm) hole in the round ends of each bone.

5 Using ¼ in. (6 mm) wide strips of black tape, attach the bones together at each end. Loop the black strip through the holes so there is a hairline space between each bone. When you have connected the last bone, you have completed the chain belt.

6 At one end of the chain belt, cut into the last hole of the bone. Insert the closed end of the key chain clip.

7 Using small pieces of tape to match each side, close the slit. Trim any excess tape around the shape of the bone.

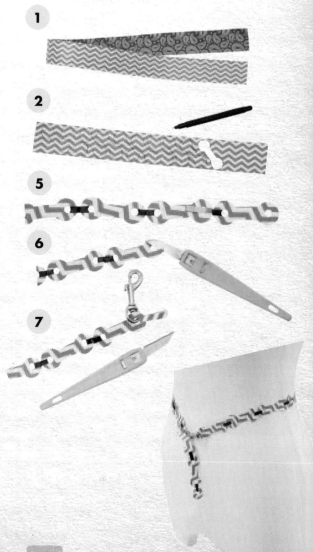

1

2

5

6

7

Materials

» Sour apple green linen duct tape
» Black and white gingham duct tape
» Silver metallic duct tape
» Metal key chain clip

Additional tools

» Circles stencil
» ¼ in. (6 mm) hole punch

47. Circle Chain Belt

1 Using sour apple green tape on one side and black and white gingham tape on the other, make two 36 in. (91 cm) double-sided strips.

2 Using the circles stencil, trace 28–32 1 ⅞ in. (4.75 cm) diameter circles (adjust to length of belt you want) on the sour apple side of the strips. Cut out the circles with scissors.

3 Using the hole punch, make two ¼ in. (6 mm) holes at opposite sides of each circle.

4 Using ¼ in. (6 mm) wide strips of silver metallic tape, attach the circles together at each end. Loop the silver strip through the holes so there is a hairline space between each circle. When you have connected the last circle, you have completed the chain belt.

5 At one end of the chain belt, cut into the last hole of the circle. Insert the closed end of the key chain clip.

6 Using small pieces of tape to match each side, close the slit. Trim any excess tape around the outer edge of the circle.

1
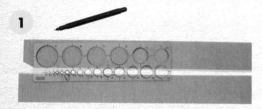

3

4

6

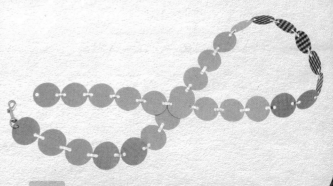

48. Crumpled Pleat Belt

1 Using Platypus® tape (it's stiffer than other tape brands and makes an excellent belt base), make a 40 in. (102 cm) double-sided strip.

2 Take two 20 in. (51 cm) strips of yellow tape and place one above the other to make a one-sided layered fabric. The bottom edge of the top strip should overlap the top edge of the bottom strip by approximately ¼ in. (6 mm).

3 Lay the belt base lengthwise on the worktable. Carefully lift up the yellow tape fabric. Starting at the right hand edge of the belt base, place the yellow tape fabric on top. As you roll the yellow fabric down from right to left, crumple it to create messy pleats.

4 Repeat steps 2 and 3 until the entire belt base is covered with crumpled yellow tape fabric.

5 Flip the belt base so the sticky side of the yellow tape fabric is face up. Fold the yellow tape fabric over the top and bottom edges of the belt base.

6 Place a 40 in. (102 cm) strip of yellow tape lengthwise along the belt base, covering the folded edges of the yellow tape fabric. Flip it over so the crumpled side is facing up. This is the main belt.

Materials

» Any color of Platypus® brand tape for base of belt
» Yellow duct tape
» Black duct tape
» Black 2 ¼ in. (5.5 cm) wide circular center bar belt buckle

Additional tools

» ⅛ in. (3 mm) hole punch

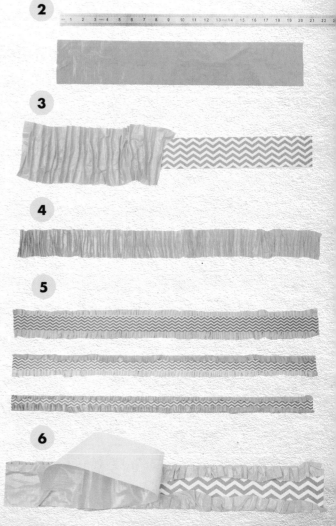

7

7 Cut a 5 in. (12.5 cm) strip of black tape and place it vertically along one end of the belt. Fold over the top and bottom ends of the black tape strip around the edge of the belt.

8 Fold the end of the belt lengthwise. Using scissors, round the corners.

8

9 Starting 2 in. (5 cm) from the outer edge, punch a row of eight holes 1 in. (2.5 cm) apart, down the center of the belt.

9

10 At the opposite end of the belt, punch a hole 1 in. (2.5 cm) in from the edge. Weave the belt through the buckle and insert the tongue through the hole. Use a piece of yellow tape to secure the end to the back of the belt.

10

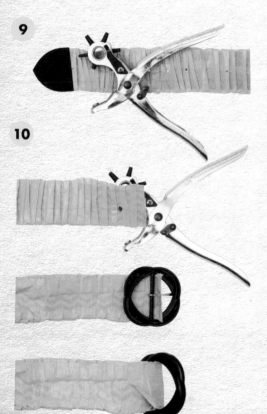

49. Rope Belt

Materials

» Silver metallic duct tape
» 3 in. (7.5 cm) strip of Velcro®

1 Cut a 22 ½ in. (57 cm) strip of tape. Cut it in half lengthwise. Fold each half strip in thirds. Trim one strip down to 20 in. (51 cm).

2 Cut a 17 ½ in. (44 cm) strip of tape. Cut it in half lengthwise. Fold each half strip in thirds. Trim one strip down to 15 in. (38 cm).

3 Cut two 3 ½ in. (9 cm) strips of tape. Position one end of the first four strips so the edges line up vertically. Place one of the 3 ½ in. (9 cm) tape strips vertically over the ends, ½ in. (1.25 cm) in from the outer edge. Fold the tape over at the top edge of the top strip and the bottom edge of the bottom strip.

4 Using the remaining 3 ½ in. (9 cm) piece of tape, repeat step 3 on the opposite ends of the four strips. This is the main part of the belt.

5 Cut a 20 in. (51 cm) strip of tape. Cut in half lengthwise. Fold each half strip in thirds. These are the side straps of the belt.

1

2

3

4

5

6

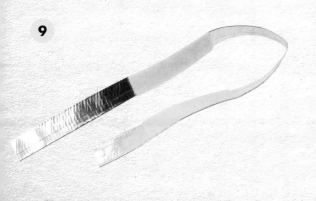

6 Attach the side straps to each end of the main belt with strips of tape and trim any excess tape. Trim one of the side straps down to 7 in. (18 cm).

7 Cut a 2 in. (5 cm) strip of tape. Cut it in half lengthwise. Fold one of the strips in thirds, and form a loop by connecting the ends with a small piece of tape.

7

8 Take the shorter side strap and pass it through the tape loop. Fold strap in half and wrap a piece of tape around it to keep the loop from falling off.

8

9 Take the longer side strap, pass 6 in. (15 cm) of it through the loop, and fold. Remove the backing from one side of the Velcro® strip. Attach it to the inside of the folded part of the strap. Then remove the other backing of the Velcro® strip and refold the strap so the adhesive sticks to the lower end.

9

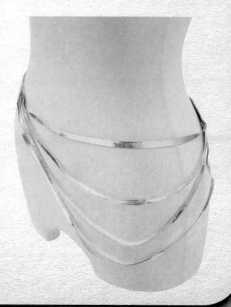

50. Wraparound Belt

Materials

» Leopard print duct tape
» Pastel yellow duct tape
» 1 in. (2.5 cm) wide center bar belt buckle

Additional tools

» ⅛ in. (3 mm) hole punch

1 Cut two 36 in. (91 cm) strips of leopard print tape. Fold both strips into thirds so they measure 1 in. (2.5 cm) wide.

2 Connect the two folded strips with a piece of leopard print tape to make one 72 in. (182 cm) piece. This is the belt.

3 Cut a 24 in. (61 cm) strip of yellow tape. Cut it lengthwise into ¼ in. (6 mm) wide strips. At one end of the belt, take one of the strips and start wrapping it around at a 45-degree angle. When the strip is done, continue with another ¼ in. (6 mm) strip and keep wrapping it around the belt until you get to the opposite end. If you run out of yellow tape, cut another set of ¼ in. (6 mm) strips.

1

2

3

4 Cut more ¼ in. (6 mm) strips of yellow tape. At one end of the belt take one of the strips and start wrapping it around at a negative 45-degree angle. You should be making "X" patterns across the belt as you intersect with the strips from step 3. Continue wrapping ¼ in. (6 mm) strips around the belt until you get to the opposite end, cutting more if necessary.

5 Cut a 36 in. (91 cm) strip of leopard print tape. Cut two ½ in. (1.25 cm) wide strips lengthwise and discard the remaining tape. Place the strips consecutively down the center of the belt. This is the front of the belt.

6 Cut a 24 in. (61 cm) strip of yellow tape. Cut it lengthwise into ¼ in. (6 mm) wide strips. Place the strips down the center of the belt, on top of the leopard strip placed in step 5.

7

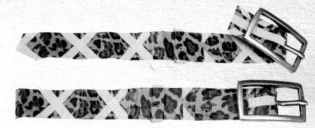

7 Take one end of the belt. Punch a
⅛ in. (3 mm) hole in the center
1 in. (2.5 cm) in from the end. Weave
that end through the belt buckle and
push the tongue through the hole. Fold
the end back and secure the buckle
to the back of the belt with a piece of
leopard print tape.

8 Take the opposite end and fold
lengthwise. Using scissors, round
the corners. Punch a row of 4–8 holes,
1 in. (2.5 cm) apart along the middle.

8

9

9 Cut a strip of yellow tape that measures
½ in. (1.25 cm) wide by 3 in. (7.5 cm)
long. Fold strip lengthwise to ¼ in. (6 mm)
wide. Wrap it around the end of the belt with
the buckle. Secure it to the back of the belt
with a piece of leopard print tape.

Materials

Materials

» Prep chevron duct tape
» Black duct tape
» 5 in. (12.5 cm) strip of Velcro®

Additional tools

» Grease pencil

51. Cummerbund

1 Using prep chevron tape on the front side and black tape on the reverse side, make a 21 in. (53 cm) wide by 5 ½ in. (14 cm) high double-sided layered fabric. Square up the edges.

2 Fold the left outer edge in half lengthwise. The folded edge should be along the bottom. From the folded corner measure and mark 1 ¼ in. (3 cm). From that point, measure 6 in. (15 cm) to the right. Angle the ruler up toward the top edge and using the grease pencil, mark the point where 6 in. (15 cm) on the ruler intersects with the top edge.

1

2

3 Using the grease pencil, draw a slightly arced line connecting the 1 ¼ in. (3 cm) mark along the left edge to the 6 in. (15 cm) mark along the top edge. Using scissors, trim along the line. Unfold the fabric.

3

4 Fold the fabric vertically so the folded edge is on the right. Using the grease pencil, trace the right side onto the left side. Use scissors to trim along the marked line, and then unfold the fabric. This is the main part of the cummerbund.

4

5 Cut a 22 in. (56 cm) strip of black tape. Place it lengthwise on the worktable with the sticky side facing up. Fold the strip lengthwise, bringing the bottom edge up ¼ in. (6 mm) from the top edge, and leaving a bit of the sticky side exposed. Flip over so the sticky side is facing down and the folded edge is along the top. Place strip on top of the cummerbund 1 in. (2.5 cm) below the top edge.

5

6 Cut a 22 in. (56 cm) strip of chevron tape. Place it lengthwise on the worktable with the sticky side facing up. Fold the strip lengthwise, bringing the bottom edge up ¼ in. (6 mm) from the top edge, and leaving a bit of the sticky side exposed. Flip over so the sticky side is facing down and the folded edge is along the top. Place strip on top of the cummerbund, ¼ in. (6 mm) below the top edge of the black strip.

7 Cut another 22 in. (56 cm) strip of black tape. Place it lengthwise on the worktable with the sticky side facing up. Fold the strip lengthwise, bringing the bottom edge up ¼ in. (6 mm) from the top edge, and leaving a bit of the sticky side exposed. Flip over so the sticky side is facing down and the folded edge is along the bottom. Place strip on top of the cummerbund 1 in. (2.5 cm) above the bottom edge.

8 Cut another 22 in. (56 cm) strip of chevron tape. Place it lengthwise on the worktable with the sticky side facing up. Fold the strip lengthwise, bringing the bottom edge up ¼ in. (6 mm) from the top edge, and leaving a bit of the sticky side exposed. Flip over so the sticky side is facing down and the folded edge is along the bottom. Place strip on top of the cummerbund ¼ in. (6 mm) above the bottom edge of the black strip.

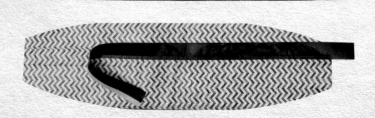

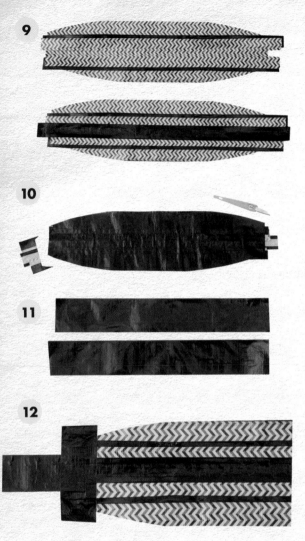

9 Cut another 22 in. (56 cm) strip of black tape. Place it on the worktable lengthwise and with the sticky side facing up. Fold the top edge down ¼ in. (6 mm). Fold the bottom edge up ¼ in. (6 mm). Flip over and place lengthwise in the center of the cummerbund.

10 Flip the cummerbund over and trim the excess tape at the other edges that fall outside the shape of the main cummerbund.

11 Make two 12 in. (30.5 cm) double-sided strips with black tape. These are the side straps.

12 Place the cummerbund on the worktable in a horizontal position. Place a side strap at each outer edge. With 5 in. (12.5 cm) strips of black tape, connect the side straps to the cummerbund. Flip the cummerbund over and place more strips of black duct tape where the straps connect. Trim the excess tape.

13 Remove the backing on one side of the Velcro® strip and place it at the end of one of the straps. Remove the other backing and attach it to the end of the other strap.

CHAPTER 4

Crazy Clothes

My first duct tape garment was a vest made for my daughter's friend Sasha. One day, when the girls were in the 5th grade, she asked me if I could make her a duct tape vest for her birthday, which was 3 months away. Of course I said yes, but then forgot about it until the actual day of her birthday party! Two hours before I had to drop off my daughter at Sasha's house, I scrambled in my studio. I had never made a vest of any sort of material before. So I found a vest in my closet and made a pattern based on its measurements. After creating the duct tape fabrics, I cut out pieces based on the pattern and connected the seams with tape. The vest was done! I added a giant "S" in hot pink on the back, wrapped it in brown craft paper, and handed the package to my daughter.

About a month later, I spotted Sasha wearing her birthday vest while running errands with her mom. When she saw me, she beamed with pride. Her vest looked great!

There are vests, skirts, and other garments in this section. For the majority of projects you will need to make a pattern, so don't skip that part! And when you do finish your garment, I hope you beam with pride—just like Sasha.

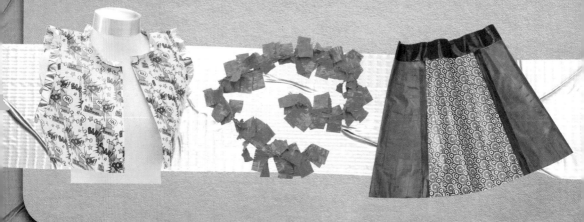

Materials

» Orange tiger paw print duct tape
» Red duct tape
» Black duct tape

Additional tools

» Grease pencil

52. Sports Bib

1 Make two 15 ¾ in. (40 cm) wide by 21 in. (53.5 cm) high double-sided layered fabrics. Use eight strips of the orange tiger paw print and five strips of black tape on the front side, and red tape on the reverse. Square up the sides.

2 Fold one of the fabrics in half vertically. At the top folded corner, mark and cut a backwards round "L" shape for the neck hole measuring at least 5 in. (12.5 cm) high and 4 in. (10 cm) wide.

3 At the open top corners, cut a rounded "L" shape for the arm hole. The cut should be at least 5 in. (12.5 cm) high and 1 ½ in. (4 cm) wide. Round off the open bottom corners. Unfold the fabric. The cut section is the straps.

4 Repeat steps 2 and 3 on the second piece of fabric.

5 Place the fabrics sideways on the worktable so the straps line up with each other but 4 in. (10 cm) apart. Connect with strips of black duct tape. Trim off any excess tape. This is the sports bib.

6 Cut two 12 in. (30.5 cm) strips of black tape. Cut each strip lengthwise in half. Fold each half strip in thirds. These are the side ties.

7 Attach the side ties to the outer edges of the sports bib with strips of red tape.

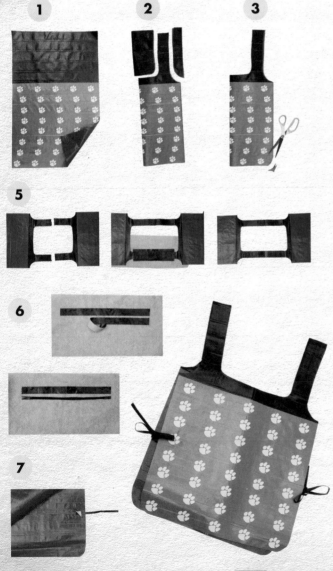

53. Work Apron

Materials

» Silver duct tape
» Denim duct tape

Additional tools

» Parchment paper

1 Begin by making a double-sided layered fabric measuring 22 in. (56 cm) wide by 11 ¼ in. (28.5 cm) high as follows: Start the fabric with a strip of silver tape and place on the worktable lengthwise with the sticky side facing up. Place a denim strip on top of the silver strip, sticky side facing down, leaving a ¼ in. (6 mm) high exposed sticky edge of the silver tape along the bottom. Pull the bottom edge of the silver tape up, creating a silver border on the denim strip. From this point on, build the fabric in the usual manner. When the denim side reaches a height of 11 ¼ in. (28.5 cm) flip over and add one strip of denim to the silver side. Flip over again so the denim side is facing up. The strip at the top should have the sticky side facing up. Place a strip of silver on top, leaving ¼ in. (6 mm) space between the top edge of the denim section and the bottom edge of the strip. Square up the sides. This is the main apron.

1

2 On a 9 in. (23 cm) wide piece of parchment paper, make two one-sided layered fabrics with silver duct tape, each measuring 8 in. (20.5 cm) wide by 6 in. (15 cm) high. Square up the sides. These are the pocket linings.

2

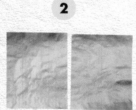

3

3 Peel back the parchment paper 1 in. (2.5 cm) at the bottom edges of the silver fabrics. Mark the center of the top edge of the apron. Place the pocket linings along the top edge of the apron, 4 in. (10 cm) apart in the center.

4

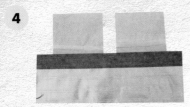

4 Flip the apron over. Place parchment paper behind the pocket linings. Remove the parchment from the pocket linings. Cover with strips of denim tape, creating a 22 in. (56 cm) wide by 7 in. (18 cm) high one-sided layered fabric on top of the silver fabric squares. Square up the sides.

5

5 Flip the apron over and remove the parchment paper. Cut an 8 in. (20.5 cm) strip of silver tape and cut in half lengthwise. Place each strip at the top edge of a pocket lining.

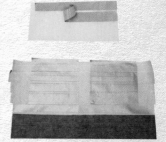

6

6 Pull the top edge down and fold at the sticky border between the denim and silver sections. Smooth down the center of the apron. Bring the outer edges of the top layer approximately ¼ in. (6 mm) inward toward the center and smooth down. This will open up the pockets.

Tape It & Wear It

7 Fold down the silver strips at the top edge of each pocket lining, to create a silver border against the denim.

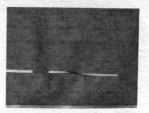

8 Cut an 11 ½ in. (29 cm) strip of silver tape and cut it in half lengthwise. Use these strips to fold over the left and right edges of the apron.

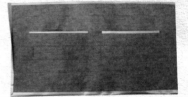

9 Fold the apron in half vertically. Using scissors, round off the bottom corners.

10 Cut a 34 in. (86 cm) strip of silver tape. Lay it on the worktable in the horizontal position. Place the top edge of the apron centered ½ in. (1.25 cm) inward from the bottom edge of the strip. Fold the strip in half lengthwise over the top edge of the apron. This is the belt of the apron.

11 Cut a 20 in. (51 cm) strip of silver tape. Lay it on the worktable in the horizontal position. Place one of the apron's belt straps on the strip along the right edge, lining up the bottom edges. Fold strip in half lengthwise over the belt strap.

12 Cut a second 20 in. (51 cm) strip of silver tape. Lay it on the worktable in the horizontal position. Place one of the apron's belt straps on the strip along the left edge and lining up the bottom edges. Fold strip in half lengthwise over the belt strap.

Materials

» Flamingo pink duct tape

54. Feather Boa

1 Make 16 double-sided strips measuring 3 in. (7.5 cm).

2 Fold each of the strips in half lengthwise. Cut slits into the open end, toward the folded end, ⅛ in. (3 mm) apart.

3 Unfold the strips and loosen the slits. At the end of each strip cut out a stem. These are the feathers.

4 Cut a 12 in. (30.5 cm) strip of tape and cut lengthwise into ¼ in. (6 mm) wide strips. Lay one of the strips on your worktable in the vertical position with the sticky side facing up. Place eight feathers on the left side and eight feathers on the right side, with the stems on the strip. The feathers should slightly overlap each other. Cover over the strip with another ¼ in. (6 mm) wide strip, sticky side facing down. This is one section of the boa.

5 Repeat steps 1–4 until you have five sections of the boa.

6 Connect the sections of the boa with strips of tape.

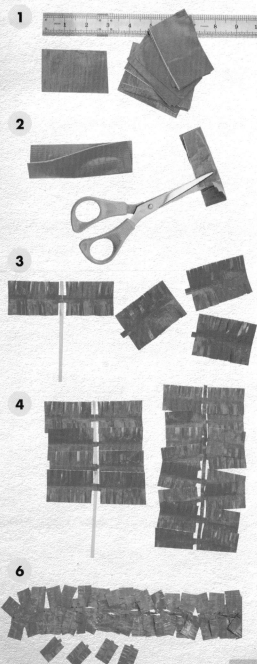

55. Vest

1 To create a vest pattern, you will need to use a tape measure to record some measurements as follows:

A: Midpoint between neck and shoulder to waist
B: A few in. (cm) below armpit to waist
C: Nape of neck to waist
D: Around the waist, divided by 4
E: Around chest, divided by 4

Use these measurements to create a vest pattern according to the diagram below.

Draw the vest pattern on newspaper or magazine paper and cut out with a craft knife. Make two patterns and tape them together at "C".

Materials

» Dark blue duct tape
» Black duct tape
» Leopard print duct tape

Additional tools

» Tape measure
» Newspaper and grease pencil

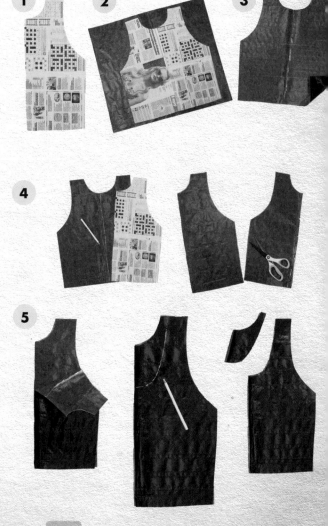

1   2   3

4

5

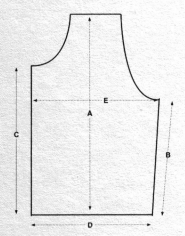

2 Using dark blue on one side and black on the other, make a double-sided layered fabric large enough to trace the vest pattern on.

3 With a grease pencil, trace the pattern onto the fabric. Remove pattern and cut out the vest shape. This is the back panel of the vest. Set aside.

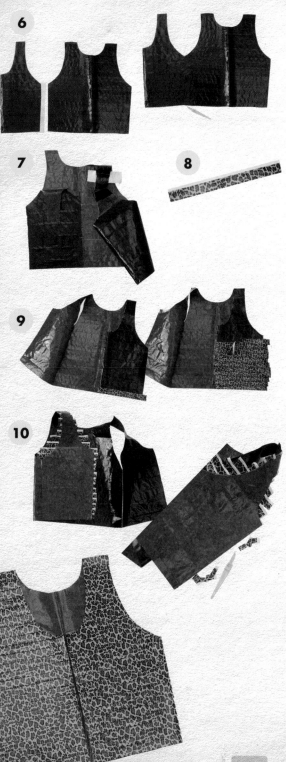

6

7

8

9

10

4 Repeat steps 2 and 3. Fold the vest pattern in half vertically and place it on the cut fabric. Line up the edges and draw down the middle of the fabric. Remove pattern and cut the fabric in half down the middle.

5 Place the two fabric halves on top of each other, lining up the edges to match. Starting at the neck, draw a deeper neckline. Cut out the neckline with scissors cutting through both layers. These are the front panels of the vest.

6 Place the back panel on the worktable with the black side facing up. Place the front panels at the sides of the back panel, matching up the seams beneath the armpit, or the "B" sides. Connect with strips of blue tape on the blue side of each panel. Trim off any excess.

7 Turn the vest right sides together, with the black side facing out. Use strips of blue tape to connect the shoulder seams, from the blue side of the panels. Trim off any excess.

8 Cut strips of leopard print tape long enough to cover the width of one front panel. Fold each strip lengthwise, pulling the bottom edge up ¼ in. (6 mm) from the top edge. There will be a border of exposed sticky side on each strip.

9 Starting at the bottom of each front panel, place the strips lengthwise, one on top of the other, overlapping by ⅛–¼ in. (3–6 mm). Cut and fold leopard print tape strips when needed until the front panels are covered.

10 Trim excess leopard print tape at the vest seams.

56. A-Line Skirt

1 To create an A-line skirt pattern, you will need to use a tape measure to record some measurements as follows:

A: Waist down to finished length, minus 2 in. (5 cm)
B: Around the waist or where you want the skirt to sit, divided by 4

Use these measurements to create a pattern similar to the diagram below.

Draw the pattern on newspaper and cut it out. Be sure the line you draw for "B" is slightly curved.

2 Using the red tape, make a double-sided layered fabric large enough to fit the skirt pattern inside. Using a grease pencil, trace the pattern onto the fabric. Use scissors to cut out the pattern shape. Repeat twice more until you have three red pattern shape pieces.

3 Using the graphic swirls tape, make a double-sided layered fabric large enough to fit the skirt pattern inside. Using a grease pencil, trace the pattern onto the fabric. Use scissors to cut out the pattern shape.

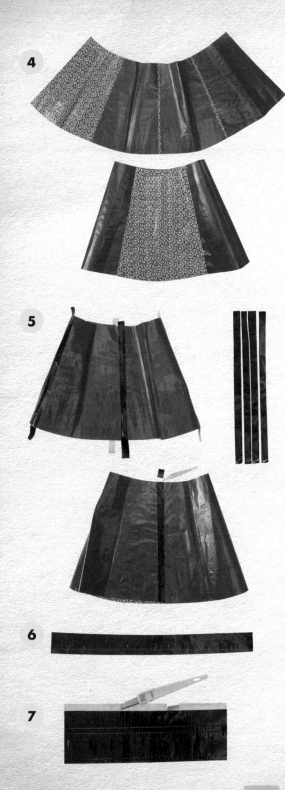

4 Using ½ in. (1.25 cm) wide strips of graphic swirl tape, connect the pieces together from the back along the side seams. Be sure to line up the waistline of all four pieces.

5 Cut two black tape strips the length of your skirt. Cut these strips in half lengthwise and use them to cover the seams from the outside. Trim off any excess tape from the top and bottom edges. This is the skirt.

6 Using the black tape, make a double-sided layered fabric that measures the same size as your waist by 3 in. (7.5 cm) high. This is the waistband.

7 Halfway along the bottom edge of the waistband, add another strip of black tape that measures the same size as your waist. Flip over so the sticky side is facing up. Cut vertical slits ½ in. (1.25 cm) apart into the sticky border.

8 Take the waistband and place the sticky border inside the waistline of the skirt so it adheres to the reverse side. The bottom edge of the waistband should meet the top edge of the skirt. Work the waistband around the skirt, pressing the sticky border against the reverse of the skirt as you go.

9

10   **11**

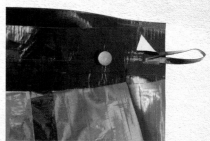

9 Starting from the back waistline, cut a vertical slit at least 10 in. (25.5 cm). Starting from the back of the waistband, 1 in. (2.5 cm) from the left edge, poke a hole using the brad of the jeans button. Take the jeans button and place it on top of the brad, then flip it over. Use the hammer to gently nail the brad into the jeans button.

10 Cut a strip of black tape at least 6 in. (15 cm) long. Cut in half lengthwise. Take one half strip and fold in thirds. This is the button loop.

11 At the back of the skirt, place the ends of the button loop inside the right edge of the waistband. Using the leftover black tape from step 10, place strips over the loop ends to hold it in place.

Materials

- » Teal duct tape
- » Cheetah kiss duct tape
- » Gold duct tape
- » Jeans button and brad

Additional tools

- » Tape measure
- » Hammer

57. Bubble Skirt

1 Use the tape measure to determine how long you want your skirt. Measure from your waist to where you want the skirt to end. This is the height of each fabric.

2 Measure your waist. This is the width of each fabric.

3 Make two double-sided layered fabrics to the measurements taken using the teal tape for the base. The cheetah kiss and gold tapes will be used for horizontal striping in the middle of the fabrics. Square up both pieces of fabric.

4 Connect the fabric pieces to make one long fabric piece. Use teal tape on the reverse side. On the front try to match the tapes on the seam. The height remains the same, but the width now will be double your waist measurement.

3

4

5

5 Starting at the left edge, measure 2 in. (5 cm) along the top edge. Vertically fold the fabric and make a 1 in. (2.5 cm) pleat. Hold the pleat in place with a piece of tape on the reverse side and a piece of teal tape folded over the top edge. Measure another 2 in. (5 cm) from the top of the pleat and vertically fold the fabric again. Make another 1 in. (2.5 cm) pleat and hold it in place with tape on the reverse side and top edge. Continue making 1 in. (2.5 cm) pleats, 2 in. (5 cm) apart, across the top edge. This is the waistline of the skirt.

6 Starting at the left edge, measure 2 in. (5 cm) along the bottom edge. Vertically fold the fabric and make a ½ in. (1.25 cm) pleat. Hold the pleat in place with a piece of tape on the reverse side and a piece of teal tape folded over the bottom edge. Measure 3 in. (7.5 cm) from the top of the pleat and vertically fold the fabric again. Make another ½ in. (1.25 cm) pleat and hold it in place with tape on the reverse side and bottom edge. Continue making ½ in. (1.25 cm) pleats, 3 in. (7.5 cm) apart across the bottom edge. This is the hemline of the skirt.

7 Connect the outer edges of the skirt with strips of tape on the back and front. Try to match the tapes on the front side of the seam.

8 Using the cheetah kiss tape, make a double-sided layered fabric the same length as your waist and 3 in. (7.5 cm) high. This is the waistband.

9 Halfway along the bottom edge of the waistband add another strip of cheetah kiss tape the same length as your waist. Flip over so the sticky side is facing up. Cut vertical slits, ½ in. (1.25 cm) apart, into the sticky border.

10 Take the waistband and place the sticky border inside the waistline of the skirt so it adheres to the reverse side. The bottom edge of the waistband should meet the waistline edge of the skirt. Work the waistband around the skirt, pressing the sticky border against the reverse side of the skirt as you go.

6

7

8

9

10

11 11 Starting from the waistline at the back of the skirt, cut a vertical slit at least 10 in. (25 cm) long. Cover the sides of the opening with strips of teal tape.

12 Measure 1 in. (2.5 cm) from the left edge and starting from the back of the waistband, poke a hole using the brad of the jeans button. Take the jeans button and place it on top of the brad, then flip it over. Use the hammer to gently nail the brad into the jeans button.

11

13 Cut a strip of cheetah tape at least 6 in. (15 cm) long. Cut in half lengthwise. Take one of the half strips and fold in thirds. This is the button loop.

14 At the back of the skirt, place the ends of the button loop inside the right edge of the waistband. Place strips over the loop ends to hold it in place.

58. String Bikini Top

1 To create a string bikini top pattern, draw the diagram below on newspaper or magazine paper and cut out.

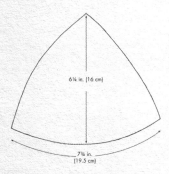

6¼ in. (16 cm)

7¾ in. (19.5 cm)

2 Make a double-sided layered fabric large enough to trace two bikini top patterns. Trace the pattern twice with a grease pencil and cut out the pieces. These are the bikini cups.

3 Cut two 8 in. (20.5 cm) strips of tape. Cut one of them in half lengthwise and set aside one of the half strips.

4 Take the full sized 8 in. (20.5 cm) strip and place it on the worktable lengthwise with the sticky side facing up. Place the half strip on top lengthwise down the center, sticky side facing down. With a craft knife, only on the half strip, make vertical slits across the middle 1 in. (2.5 cm) apart.

5 Take one of the bikini cups and line up its bottom edge to the top edge of the half strip. Fold the strip lengthwise, lining up the bottom edge of the half strip with the bottom edge of the bikini cup. Loosen up the slits. These are loops that will hold the string in step 8.

1

2

3

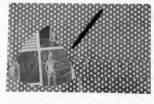

4

5

6 Cut another 8 in. (20.5 cm) strip and place it on the worktable lengthwise with the sticky side facing up. Place the remaining half strip from step 3 on top lengthwise down the center, sticky side facing down. With a craft knife, only on the half strip, make vertical slits across the middle 1 in. (2.5 cm) apart.

7 Repeat step 5 on the remaining bikini cup.

8 Cut a 36 in. (91.5 cm) strip of tape and cut it in half lengthwise. Fold each strip into ¼ in. (6 mm) wide strings.

8

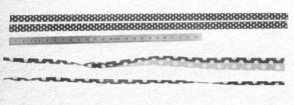

9 Pass one string through the loops at the bottom of each bikini cup. Then connect the strings with a piece of tape.

10 Cut a 20 in. (51 cm) strip of tape and cut it in half lengthwise. Fold each strip into ¼ in. (6 mm) wide strings.

11 Attach one string to the top of each bikini cup with a piece of tape.

9

11

59. Bodice

Materials

- » Punk rock duct tape
- » White duct tape
- » Black duct tape
- » Velcro® strip measuring "C"

Additional tools

- » Tape measure
- » Newspaper and grease pencil

1 To create the two bodice patterns, you will need to use a tape measure to record some measurements as follows:

A: Mid back to waist
B: Around the waist, divided by 4
C: A few in. (cm) below armpit to waist
D: Mid breast bone to waist
Use these measurements to create a bodice pattern according to the diagram below.

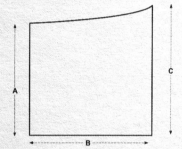

The top pattern is for the back panel. Using the measurements above, draw two of these back panel patterns on newspaper and cut out. Connect with tape at "A".

The bottom pattern is for the front panel. Using the measurements above, draw two of these front panel patterns on newspaper and cut out. Connect with tape at "D".

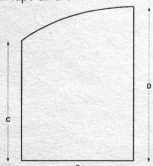

1

2

3

4

5

6

7

2 Make a double-sided layered fabric large enough to fit the back panel pattern inside. Use punk rock tape on the front side and white tape on the reverse side. Trace the pattern on the fabric with the grease pencil and cut out.

3 Make a double-sided layered fabric large enough to fit the front panel pattern inside. Use punk rock and black tapes on the front side, and white tape on the reverse side. Stripe the tape strips on the front side vertically. Trace the pattern on the fabric with the grease pencil and cut out.

4 Place the fabric panels on the work-table, the white side facing up. Line up the "C" edge of the front panel with the "C" edge of the back panel. Connect with a piece of white tape. This is the bodice.

5 Place a piece of white tape along the remaining "C" side of the front panel. Put the bodice around your torso. Close up the side seam (this is only temporary). Beneath your chest pull in the extra fabric and make two equally sized vertical folds. Hold the folds with small pieces of tape that you will remove later on.

6 Undo the tape on the side seam and remove the bodice. Place it on the worktable with the white side facing up, and use remaining pieces of white tape from step 5 to secure the folds.

7 Cut a 4 in. (10 cm) vertical slit down the middle of the front panel. Fold the front panel vertically in half. Use scissors to round off the top corners of the slit.

8 Open seam from step 5 and place Velcro® strip along edges of both sides. This is the bodice closure.

60. Bolero Vest

Materials

» Electric blue duct tape
» Silver metallic duct tape
» Comic book duct tape

Additional tools

» Newspaper and grease pencil

1 To create a vest pattern, you will need to use a tape measure to record some measurements as follows.

A: Midpoint between neck and shoulder to mid-abdomen height
B: A few in. (cm) below armpit to mid-abdomen height
C: Nape of neck to mid-abdomen height
D: Around the mid-abdomen, divided by 4
E: Around chest, divided by 4
Use these measurements to create a bolero vest pattern according to the diagram below.

Draw pattern on newspaper or magazine paper and cut out with a craft knife. Make two patterns and tape them together at "C".

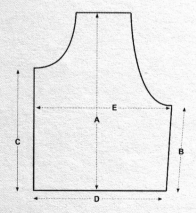

2 Make a double-sided layered fabric large enough to trace the bolero pattern on. Use electric blue on one side and silver metallic on the other.

3 Using a grease pencil, trace the pattern onto the fabric.

1

2

3

4

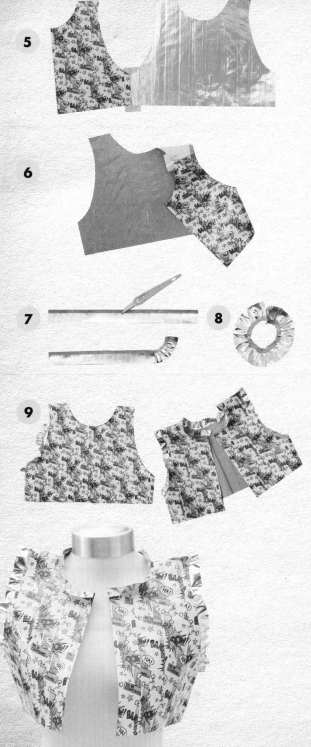

Remove pattern and cut out the vest shape. This is the back panel of the vest. Set aside.

4 Repeat steps 2 and 3, using comic book tape on one side and electric blue on the other. Fold the vest pattern in half vertically and place it on the cut fabric. Line up the edges and draw down the middle of the fabric. Remove pattern and cut the fabric in half down the middle. These are the front panels of the vest.

5 Place the back panel on the worktable with the silver side facing up. Place the front panels at the sides of the back panel, matching up the seams beneath the armpit, or the "B" sides. The comic book sides of the front panels should be facing up. Connect with strips of blue tape on the reverse side of each seam. Trim off any excess.

6 Use strips of blue tape to connect the shoulder seams on the reverse. Trim off any excess.

7 Cut at least five 12 in. (30.5 cm) strips of silver print tape. Fold each strip lengthwise, pulling the bottom edge up ¼ in. (6 mm) from the top edge. There should be a border of exposed sticky side on each strip. Cut vertical slits ½ in. (1.25 cm) long and ½ in. (1.25 cm) apart into the sticky border.

8 At each slit pull the sides together so they overlap. These are the ruffles.

9 Place the sticky edges of each strip of ruffles along the inside of the neckline and armhole lines.

Online Resources

General Materials:
Uline, *www.uline.com*

General Art and Craft Supplies:
A. I. Friedman, *www.aifriedman.com*
Amazon, *www.amazon.com*
Dick Blick Art Materials, *www.dickblick.com*
Jerry's Artarama, *www.jerrysartarama.com*
Michaels, *www.michaels.com*
Pearl Fine Art Supplies, *www.pearlpaint.com*
Tape Brothers, *www.tapebrothers.com*
Utrecht Art Supplies, *www.utrechtart.com*

Trimming:
M&J Trimming, *www.mjtrim.com*
Trim Fabric, *www.trimfabric.com*

Sewing and Quilting Supplies:
Home-Sew Inc., *www.homesew.com*
Sew True, *www.sewtrue.com*

Duct Tape Brands and Manufacturers:
3M, *www.3m.com*
Duck™ brand tape *www.duckbrand.com*
Nashua, *www.nashua.com*
Platypus® Designer Duct Tape™,
www.designerducttape.com

Hair Accessories:
Factory Direct Craft, *www.factorydirectcraft.com*

Acknowledgments

Writing and crafting can be lonely, so I'd like to thank those who made me feel a little less isolated. My friend Charise carved out time for me despite being one of the busiest writers/artists I know. My sisters Chonaliza and Elleanore ensured I never took myself too seriously. Friends Hallie, Susan, Ann, Francine, and Rosy advised me on editorial issues. My cousin Mike shared his "wisdom" via text, reinforcing the fact that he is the funniest person I know.

I'd also like to thank Caroline Elliker, Mark Searle, Ellie Wilson, and Gareth Butterworth at Quintet, who made everything I do look better. Eric Lowenhar, Jackie Raab, and Ellen Sibley at Barron's Educational Series paved the way to continued success. Kate McKean at Howard Morhaim Literary Agency gave me great advice when I needed it most.

Michael Joseph Lia, I dedicate this book to you. I promised this when you were only eight years old, and now you are 13, and your enthusiasm and belief in me remains unchanged. I hope that Aunt Richela never disappoints you!

About the author

Richela Fabian Morgan began her duct tape odyssey seven years ago with a simple bi-fold wallet, before writing *Tape It & Make It* and *Tape It & Make More*. She is an indie crafter specializing in paper, adhesives, and found materials, and has taught various craft projects at elementary schools, public libraries, and charitable organizations around the US. She has written several books and blogs regularly on *richelafabianmorgan.com*. Richela lives in Larchmont, New York, with her husband and two crafty kids.